Neo-Georgian Fiction

This book contributes to the development of contemporary historical fiction studies with new analyses of neo-Georgian fiction, which, unlike neo-Victorian fiction, until now has received little critical attention. The essays included in this collection study the ways in which selected twentieth- and twenty-first-century novels recreate the Georgian period in order to view its ideologies through the lens of such modern critical theories as performativity, post-colonialism, feminism or visual theories. They also demonstrate the rich repertoire of subgenres of neo-Georgian fiction, ranging from biographical fiction, epistolary novels to magical realism. The studies of the diverse novelistic conventions used to recontextualise the Georgian reality reflect the way we see its relevance and relation to the present and trace the indebtedness of the new forms of the contemporary novel to the traditional novelistic genres.

Jakub Lipski is Associate Professor of Anglophone Literatures at Kazimierz Wielki University in Bydgoszcz, Poland. His research interests include eighteenth-century English fiction and culture, the correspondences between word and image, and reception and adaptation studies. He is the author of *In Quest of the Self: Masquerade and Travel in the Eighteenth-Century Novel* (2014), *Painting the Novel: Pictorial Discourse in Eighteenth-Century English Fiction* (2018) and editor of *Rewriting Crusoe: The Robinsonade across Languages, Cultures, and Media* (2020).

Joanna Maciulewicz is Associate Professor in the Department of English Literature and Literary Linguistics, Adam Mickiewicz University, Poznań, Poland. She is the author of *Representations of Book Culture in Eighteenth-Century English Imaginative Writing* (2018). Her research interests focus on eighteenth-century literature and culture, the history of the book and the theory of early English, Spanish and Polish fiction. She is an assistant editor of *Studia Anglica Posnaniensia*.

Routledge Focus on Literature

Neo-Georgian Fiction
Reimagining the Eighteenth Century in the Contemporary
Historical Novel
Edited by Jakub Lipski and Joanna Maciulewicz

Introduction to Digital Humanities
Enhancing Scholarship with the Use of Technology
Kathryn C. Wymer

Geomythology
How Common Stories are Related to Earth Events
Timothy J. Burbery

Re-Reading the Eighteenth-Century Novel
Studies in Reception
Jakub Lipski

Trump and Autobiography
Corporate Culture, Political Rhetoric, and Interpretation
Nicholas K. Mohlmann

Biofictions
Literary and Visual Imagination in the Age of Biotechnology
Lejla Kucukalic

Neurocognitive Interpretations of Australian Literature
Criticism in the Age of Neuroawareness
Jean-François Vernay

For more information about this series, please visit: www.routledge.
com/Routledge-Focus-on-Literature/book-series/RFLT

Neo-Georgian Fiction

Reimagining the Eighteenth Century
in the Contemporary Historical Novel

**Edited by Jakub Lipski and
Joanna Maciulewicz**

Routledge
Taylor & Francis Group

NEW YORK AND LONDON

First published 2021
by Routledge
605 Third Avenue, New York, NY 10017

and by Routledge
2 Park Square, Milton Park, Abingdon, Oxon OX14 4RN

Routledge is an imprint of the Taylor & Francis Group, an informa business

Library of Congress Cataloging-in-Publication Data
Names: Lipski, Jakub, editor. | Maciulewicz, Joanna, editor.
Title: Neo-Georgian fiction: reimagining the eighteenth century in the contemporary historical novel / edited by Jakub Lipski and Joanna Maciulewicz.
Description: New York, NY: Routledge, 2021. |
Series: Routledge focus on literature |
Includes bibliographical references and index.
Identifiers: LCCN 2020053795 (print) | LCCN 2020053796 (ebook)
Subjects: LCSH: Historical fiction, English–History and criticism. |
English fiction–20th century–History and criticism. | English fiction–
21st century–History and criticism. | Great Britain–In literature.
Classification: LCC PR888.H5 N46 2021 (print) |
LCC PR888.H5 (ebook) | DDC 823/.08109–dc23
LC record available at https://lccn.loc.gov/2020053795
LC ebook record available at https://lccn.loc.gov/2020053796

ISBN 13: 978-0-367-43014-6 (hbk)
ISBN 13: 978-1-03-200389-4 (pbk)

Typeset in Times New Roman
by Newgen Publishing UK

Contents

Illustrations

Contributors

Tymon Adamczewski is Assistant Professor in the Department of Anglophone Literatures, Kazimierz Wielki University in Bydgoszcz, Poland. His academic interests revolve around the critical discourses of contemporary humanities, music and ecocriticism. He is the author of *Following the Textual Revolution: The Standardization of Radical Critical Theories of the 1960s* (2016) and has recently edited the volume *Bob Dylan: America and the World* (2020).

Daniel Cook is Reader in English and Associate Director of The Centre for Scottish Culture at the University of Dundee in Scotland. He has published widely on eighteenth- and nineteenth-century British and Irish literature, with a particular focus on Jonathan Swift and his circle. His books include *Walter Scott and Short Fiction* (2021), *Reading Swift's Poetry* (2020), *Thomas Chatterton and Neglected Genius, 1760–1830* (2013), *Women's Life Writing, 1700–1850: Gender, Genre and Authorship* (2012, with Amy Culley), and *The Afterlives of Eighteenth-Century Fiction* (2015, with Nicholas Seager).

Jakub Lipski is Associate Professor of Anglophone Literatures at Kazimierz Wielki University in Bydgoszcz, Poland. His research interests include eighteenth-century English fiction and culture, the correspondences between word and image, and reception and adaptation studies. He is the author of *In Quest of the Self: Masquerade and Travel in the Eighteenth-Century Novel* (2014), *Painting the Novel: Pictorial Discourse in Eighteenth-Century English Fiction* (2018) and editor of *Rewriting Crusoe: The Robinsonade across Languages, Cultures, and Media* (2020).

Joanna Maciulewicz is Associate Professor in the Department of English Literature and Literary Linguistics, Adam Mickiewicz University, Poznań, Poland. She is the author of *Representations* *of Book Culture in Eighteenth-Century English Imaginative Writing* (2018). Her research interests focus on eighteenth-century literature and culture, the history of the book and the theory of early English, Spanish and Polish fiction. She is an assistant editor of *Studia Anglica Posnaniensia.*

M-C. Newbould teaches and researches eighteenth-century literature and visual culture at the University of Cambridge, where she is a Senior Research Associate at the Faculty of English and a Bye-Fellow of Pembroke College. Mary's research interests principally revolve around Laurence Sterne's work and its afterlives. Her *Adaptations of Laurence Sterne's Fiction: Sterneana, 1760–1840* was published in 2013, and she is currently creating a database hosted by Cambridge Digital Library to make this material freely available to a global audience.

Przemysław Uściński is Assistant Professor at the Institute of English Studies, University of Warsaw. He has published a number of articles on British literature and culture of the eighteenth century, the history and criticism of the novel, the aesthetics of satire, parody and translation. His book *Parody, Scriblerian Wit and the Rise of the Novel* was published in 2016, and his current research focuses on the theories of hypocrisy and disavowal, English urban satire, and the eighteenth-century sentimental novel.

Introduction

Delineating the Neo-Georgian

Jakub Lipski and Joanna Maciulewicz

In the most recent issue of *The Rambling*, leading scholars of eighteenth-century studies ponder the possible directions in which research in the field can develop and express a belief in the continuing relevance of the period's legacies for our understanding of the present. Jonathan Sachs, in his introductory essay, gives the examples of the revived interest in Daniel Defoe's *A Journal of the Plague Year* (1722) in the context of the Covid-19 pandemic and the overthrowing of the statue of slave trader Edward Colston in Bristol, and argues that these two events serve as "a reminder […] of two larger and longer episodes that center on the eighteenth century: the development of the novel as a form, and the legacy of the slave trade", which "contribute to [other] close-related legacies".[1] In Daniel Defoe's factual/novelistic plague journal, readers discover their own Covid-19 experience and the protests related to the Black Lives Matter movement provoke debates on the lingering effects of slavery in the twenty-first century. One could add the recent rereadings of Samuel Richardson's *Pamela* in the light of the #MeToo movement,[2] the uses of Robinsonade iconography in the Brexit debate,[3] references to Jonathan Swift's *Gulliver's Travels* in critical evaluations of Donald Trump's politics,[4] and the popularity of such TV shows as *Outlander* (2014–), *Black Sails* (2014–2017) and *Harlots* (2017–2019), representing eighteenth-century realities in accord with the cultural, social and political preoccupations of our own time. "The eighteenth century, we might therefore argue, is more relevant than ever. Indeed, […] the eighteenth century isn't over yet", as Sachs concludes his essays.[5]

The interest in eighteenth-century legacies is manifest also in contemporary historical novels set in the Georgian era. Elodie Rousselot labels this kind of fiction neo-Georgian and classifies it as one of the variants of the neo-historical novel, the most recently developed subgenre of the historical novel.[6] She argues that, just like other kinds of contemporary historical fiction, it aims to explore the nature of the relationship between the present and the past, but, unlike historiographic metafiction, which employs self-reflexive commentary to expose the limitations of historical writing, the neo-historical novel returns to verisimilitude in its representations of the past. This does not mean that it abjures the critical approach of postmodernist historical fiction. Rather than employing "an overtly disruptive mode", it "carries out its potential for radical possibilities in more implicit ways".[7]

Rousselot's foregrounding of the neo-historical novel as the latest stage in the development of historical fiction, distinct from historiographic metafiction, does not cohere, however, with the growing conviction that the critical practice of classifying historical fiction in accordance with "the moment of production" rather than "the era that is revived within the novels"[8] does not do justice to the complexity of the genre. "Historical fiction", Louisa Hadley argues, "is defined as much by the period it evokes as by the period it is written in", since, by its very nature, it is characterised by "a dual approach which combines a concern with the past and with the present".[9] Such an approach legitimates studying neo-Tudor, neo-Georgian or neo-Victorian fiction as distinct subgenres rather than as mere variants of the postmodernist or the neo-historical novel. This kind of thinking is supported, for instance, by Dana Shiller, who defines neo-Victorian fiction as "a subset of the historical novel" that is "at once characteristic of postmodernism and imbued with a historicity reminiscent of the nineteenth-century novel".[10] Donna Heiland makes a similar point when she argues, albeit without using the term neo-Georgian, that the "works set in, or in some way dealing with, the long eighteenth century [...] constitute a genuine literary subgenre"[11] that should be studied as an independent literary phenomenon. Treating such texts merely as examples of postmodernist or postcolonial fiction, without acknowledging their specificity, "would only scratch the difference of their accomplishment".[12] In this volume we attempt a closer delineation of neo-Georgian fiction, with the essays included showing the diversity of historiographic conventions adopted in this subgenre: Chapters 1 and 2 discuss novels traditionally classified as examples of historiographic metafiction while Chapters 3–6 offer focused readings of more recent texts, which, without renouncing the self-critical gaze, are more verisimilar in nature.

Our analyses of various forms of neo-Georgian fiction add to the recent scholarship on the historical novel, a genre which for the last few decades has been enjoying a noticeable revival. Jerome de Groot described it as "the most important, influential and enduring literary genre of the last thirty five years".[13] Its significance and vitality is evidenced not only by the presence of numerous historical novels on the winners' lists of prestigious literary awards, including double Booker-winning neo-Tudor narratives by Hilary Mantel, but also by the creation, in 2009, of the Sir Walter Scott Prize for Historical Fiction, one of the richest literary awards in the UK, which, in the words of Mantel, aims to "push writers on to explore the limits of technique and the limits of their influence".[14] The stimulus for the regeneration of the genre came from postmodernist fiction, which openly and self-consciously explored the coexistence of history and fiction, most memorably perhaps in John Barth's *The Sot-Weed Factor* (1960) and John Fowles's *The French Lieutenant's Woman* (1969). If in 1980 the genre still "seemed in a moribund state" and "was generally considered to be conservative and stale",[15] the following decades, with the widely popular and creatively innovative historical narratives by such authors as Peter Ackroyd, Jeanette Winterson and A.S. Byatt, saw its gradual rise both in terms of popular appeal and critical acclaim. The foregrounding of the metafictional strain in the postmodernist historical novel encouraged critics to look at the development of the genre from a fresh perspective, which has led to conclusions that make us reconsider its nature and origin. Going beyond the traditional critical narrative about Walter Scott as the "father" of the historical novel, some recent criticism has suggested that the interrelation of the historical and the fictional in historical fiction is nothing but a continuation of the early novels' self-reflexive analysis of its own affinity with historical writing. As Robert Mayer argues, because "[h]istory was the one discourse that virtually all seventeenth- and eighteenth-century fiction writers [...] identified as the matrix of their fiction", the novel is a genre which by its very nature "forces the history-fiction problematic on the reader in a way that no other fictional discourse does".[16] Kate Mitchell and Nicola Parson echo this observation, claiming that eighteenth-century "readers and authors had a more nuanced understanding of fiction's relationship to history"[17] than was previously believed. Anne Stevens develops the idea, arguing that it is legitimate to look for historical novels as early as in the eighteenth century.[18]

The critical strain of the contemporary historical novel, inherent also in the forms of the genre developed in the earlier periods, has now been successfully theorized in the criticism of neo-Victorian fiction, which has been set apart as a distinct genre and a separate area of research in the broader field of Victorian studies. Neo-Victorian novels, as Ann Heilmann and Mark Llewellyn argue, are "*self-consciously engaged with the act of (re)interpretation, (re)discovery and (re)vision concerning the Victorians*" (original emphasis).[19] A faithful recreation of the Victorian era is never an aim in itself; rather, invoking the past becomes a strategy of "answering the needs and preoccupations of the present"[20] or even "negotiating the shape of the present".[21] This does not mean that neo-Victorian fiction renounces the ambition to portray the past; on the contrary, it typically abounds in circumstantial descriptions of Victorian customs, manners and material culture based on thorough research into the period. This period reconstruction, however, is likely to be read and reinterpreted through the lens of contemporary critical theories, including feminism, psychoanalysis or postcolonialism, in an attempt to address the major problems of the present, most frequently those of gender, sexuality, race or empire, or, alternatively, to reveal those aspects of Victorian life that, due to moral censorship, could not be explicitly described.

That said, the neo-Victorian remains elusive to attempts at stricter conceptualisation. One of the reasons may be the wealth of forms that it has generated. As Cora Kaplan points out, neo-Victorian fiction "has colonised or invented" many genres that engaged with "the Victorian through a mix of narrative strategies".[22] Multifarious kinds of neo-Victorian fiction have been described and commented upon. Kate Mitchell distinguishes those that retell the stories of significant historical events, "ventriloquise Victorian writers", rewrite the plots of classic Victorian novels, or supplement them with sequels or prequels.[23] Sally Shuttleworth argues that we may talk about such types as "low-life and underworld, lesbian sexuality or psychiatry".[24] Robin Gilmour claims that we can also classify neo-Victorian fiction in accordance with the uses to which it puts the past. There are novels that rewrite the Victorian past from the modern perspective but without much narratorial interference, pastiches and parodies, narratives that subvert the period's ideology, novels that abuse Victorian novelistic conventions, the rewritings of Victorian classic novels and the so-called research novels.[25]

There is also the controversial question of the origin of neo-Victorian fiction. Most scholars associate the emergence of the neo-Victorian, "somewhat too simplistically",[26] with the publication of Jean Rhys's *Wide Sargasso Sea* (1966) and John Fowles's *The French Lieutenant's Woman* (1969), but Victorianism's afterlife in fiction began as soon as the period was over. The following eras used it as a foil useful for shaping their own ideas, values or forms of expression. From the "marginalisation of the Victorian past at the outset of the twentieth century"[27] to the celebration of the "Victorian Values—thrift, family, enterprise"[28] in 1980s and 1990s, the responses to Victorian legacies ranged from "simultaneous abjection from and attraction to the Victorian".[29] It is more productive then, as Marie-Luise Kohlke suggests, to talk about the "crucial nodal points in neo-Victorian output"[30] than to strive to find its exact point of origin.

The background of this burgeoning neo-Victorianism may be very useful for a more methodical reflection on neo-Georgian fiction, not only here, but – hopefully – in the years to come. Although recent decades have seen the publication of numerous novels set in the eighteenth century, they have received far less critical attention than the fiction set a century later and there have been no systematic attempts to describe them as a specific subgenre of historical fiction and the ways they explore the relationship between the Georgian past and the present, with the notable exception of the previously mentioned essay by Donna Heiland, who does not, however, use a generic label for these novels. More than two decades have gone by and no such label has settled for good in criticism.

Our use of the term neo-Georgian and the idea to promote it may appear controversial on several levels. First, while the reign of Queen Victoria (1837–1901) has long been typically identified with a historical, literary and socio-cultural "period" – the Victorian period, it would be difficult to ascribe the same kind of "period identity" to the reigns of the four Georges (1714–1837), especially as there are normally different ideas for periodisation among eighteenth-century studies scholars, with the "long eighteenth century" sometimes extending from 1650 to 1850. Second, the final four decades of the Georgian period, 1795–1837, have been understood to have manifested their own identity as the Regency period. The popularity of "neo-Regency" cultural productions, such as the numerous rereadings and imitations of Jane Austen, is – in our opinion – a separate cultural phenomenon, beyond this volume's use and understanding of the "neo-Georgian". Third, rarely invoked in literary studies, the term "neo-Georgian" has a relatively long history of usage with reference to architecture, designating a revival of interest in Georgian architectural forms in the first decades of the twentieth century.

Why "neo-Georgian", then? For one thing, it has been used before, by Elodie Rousselot, even if in a slightly narrower sense. As mentioned above, Rousselot uses other similar terms by way of analogy, such as "neo-Tudor", and this labelling seems consistent and orderly. For another thing, it acquires significance by virtue of the immediate associations with the neo-Victorian, and this is indeed the effect we wish to achieve here, arguing – collectively and in each of the separate chapters – that contemporary historical fiction set in the eighteenth century does the same socio-cultural work as neo-Victorian fiction; that is, it actualises and revisions the Georgian past to comment on what is topical and relevant today. Some of these concerns, such as gender, race and empire, have been tackled in neo-Georgian fiction in a manner that is reminiscent of how they have been explored in neo-Victorian fiction. Others are more period specific, including issues of professional literary market, authorship or explorations of the affinity between fact and fiction.

The genealogy of the neo-Georgian goes back almost to the final years of the Georgian period itself, with Walter Scott trying to shape the Scotland of his own time by summoning the eighteenth-century lore and William Makepeace Thackeray playing with the Fieldingesque convention and the clash of micro- and macro-history in *The Luck of Barry Lyndon* (1844). Charles Dickens's *A Tale of Two Cities* (1859) and R. L. Stevenson's *Treasure Island* (1883), in turn, show how eighteenth-century content resonated with the Victorian ideologies of class and empire. Past-oriented fiction invariably represents the problems of the past in relation to its own concerns, exploring the ways it affected its own ideas, forms of writing or artistic expression, and, accordingly, it is best studied from the perspective of the here and now. Thus, rather than offering a genealogical narrative of the neo-Georgian, we focus in this volume on how contemporary novels revive eighteenth-century themes, such as the masquerade, literary marketplace and authorship, slave trade, prostitution and commercialisation, visuality, epistolarity, libertinism and science, to offer historicised perspectives on the problems causing anxiety at present.

What follows cannot possibly offer a full picture of neo-Georgian fiction today; it is our hope, nevertheless, that the subsequent focused readings of selected late twentieth- and twenty-first-century novels by both canonical and lesser-known authors successfully sketch the perimeters of a research field that will attract attention. To this end, our agenda has been twofold: to demonstrate the relevance of Georgian concerns today and to determine the generic identity of the neo-Georgian by emphasising contemporary appropriations of period-specific material; in other words, to show why certain topical concerns of our own time are best addressed by summoning the Georgian past. In Chapter 1, Jakub Lipski's reading of Peter Ackroyd's neo-Georgian fiction shows how Enlightenment philosophies of personal identity and the Georgian obsession with masquerading and theatre can elucidate modern debates about performativity and the self. In the following chapter, Daniel Cook studies two appearances of Daniel Defoe as fictional character, in J.M. Coetzee's *Foe* (1986) and Stuart Campbell's *Daniel Defoe's Railway Journey* (2017), to ponder more general questions about discursive power and narrative authority in the context of the mechanisms of the Georgian literary marketplace and the evolving notion of authorship. Przemysław Uściński (Chapter 3) reads Barry Unsworth's *Sacred Hunger* (1992) and argues that the eighteenth-century slave trade realities are invoked in the novel to address wider concerns about the coercive and disciplining dimensions of economic systems. Uściński makes use of the contemporary criticism of the so-called "terracentric history", reading Unsworth's novel also as a reflection on how Georgian sea affairs shaped modernity. M-C. Newbould, in Chapter 4, focuses on two recent novels re-visioning William Hogarth's famous cycle *A Harlot's Progress* and the ways in which they bring in questions of race and gender to problematise aspects of spectacle and visual culture along the lines of the marginalisation/inclusivity dialectic. In Chapter 5, Tymon Adamczewski offers a close reading of Michael Irwin's 2013 *The Skull and the Nightingale*, and argues that the novel's traditional epistolary format in a metafictional sense, provokes more general questions about the nature of reading as vicarious experience – an understanding of fiction that was also implied by a number of Georgian works, from epistolary fictions to quixotic narratives and sentimental reenactments of feeling. Finally, in the concluding chapter, Joanna Maciulewicz analyses Imogen Hermes Gowar's magical realist novel *The Mermaid and Mrs Hancock* to explore the way it uses the conventions ousted from the novelistic tradition in its depiction of the predicament of women in the period of the rapid commercialisation of social life and the affinity between imaginative and scientific discourses in the eighteenth century. Far from exhausting the field, these chapters nevertheless indicate some of the crucial points of convergence between the Georgian period and the broadly understood here and now. In doing so, they also delineate, albeit tentatively, the specificity of the neo-Georgian and its identity as an autonomous field within the wider panorama of contemporary historical fiction.

Notes

1 Jonathan Sachs, "The Future of the Eighteenth Century", *The Rambling* 9 (2020), https://the-rambling.com/2020/08/07/issue9-sachs/.

2 See, for example, Chloe Wigston Smith, "How harassed women had their #MeToo moments in the 18th century", *The Conversation* (26 February 2018), https://theconversation.com/how-harassed-women-had-their-metoo-moments-in-the-18th-century-91761, and Diana Rosenberger, "Virtual Rewarded: What #MeToo Can Learn from Samuel Richardson's *Pamela*", *South Central Review* 36.2 (2019): 17–32.

3 Robert Clark, "Robinsonade and Brexit: Free Trade, Empire and the Whole World", in *300 Years of Robinsonades*, ed. Emanuelle Peraldo (Newcastle: Cambridge Scholars Publishing, 2020), 165–189.

4 As visible in Olga Hofmann's painting *Gulliver* Trump in the Divided Land of Lillipublicans and Blefucrats (2016) used on the cover of and discussed

in the introduction to *Swiftian Inspirations: The Legacy of Jonathan Swift from the Enlightenment to the Age of Post-Truth*, ed. Jonathan McCreedy, Vesselin M. Budakov and Alexandra K. Glavanakova (Newcastle: Cambridge Scholars Publishing, 2020).

5 Jonathan Sachs, "The Future of the Eighteenth Century".

6 Elodie Rousselot, "Introduction: Exoticising the Past in Contemporary Neo-Historical Fiction", in *Exoticizing the Past in Contemporary Neo-Historical Fiction*, ed. Elodie Rousselot (Houndmills: Palgrave Macmillan, 2014), 2.

7 Rousselot, "Introduction", 5.

8 Louisa Hadley, *Neo-Victorian Fiction and Historical Narrative. The Victorians and Us* (Houndmills: Palgrave Macmillan, 2010), 5.

9 Hadley, *Neo-Victorian Fiction and Historical Narrative*, 6.

10 Dana Shiller, "The Redemptive Past in the Neo-Victorian Novel", *Studies in the Novel* 29.4 (1997): 538.

11 Donna Heiland, "Historical Subjects: Recent Fictions about the Eighteenth Century", *Eighteenth-Century Life* (1997): 108–122.

12 Heiland, "Historical Subjects", 109.

13 Jerome de Groot, "Transgression and Experimentation: The Historical Novel", in *The Cambridge Companion to British Fiction: 1980-2018*, ed. Peter Boxall (Cambridge: Cambridge University Press, 2018), 169.

14 www.walterscottprize.co.uk/about-the-prize/background/

15 De Groot, "Transgression and Experimentation", 170.

16 Robert Mayer, *History and the Early English Novel. Matters of Fact from Bacon to Defoe* (1997; Cambridge: Cambridge University Press, 2004), 15.

17 Kate Mitchell and Nicola Parson, "Reading the Represented Past: History and Fiction from 1700 to the Present", in *Reading Historical Fiction: The Revenant and Remembered Past*, ed. Kate Mitchell and Nicola Parson (Houndmills: Palgrave Macmillan, 2013), 3.

18 Anne H. Stevens, *British Historical Fiction before Scott* (Houndmills: Palgrave Macmillan, 2010), 2.

19 Ann Heilmann and Mark Llewellyn, *Neo-Victorianism. The Victorians in the Twenty-First Century* (Houndmills: Palgrave Macmillan, 2010), 4.

20 Rousselot, "Introduction", 5.

21 Heilmann and Llewellyn, *Neo-Victorianism*, 3.

22 Cora Kaplan, *Victoriana: Histories, Fiction, Criticism* (Edinburgh: Edinburgh University Press, 2007), 3, 8.

23 Kate Mitchell, *History and Cultural Memory in Neo-Victorian Fiction. Victorian Afterimages* (Houndmills: Palgrave Macmillan, 2010), 2.

24 Sally Shuttleworth, "From Retro- to Neo-Victorian Fiction and Beyond: Fearful Symmetries", in *Neo-Victorian Literature and Culture: Immersions and Revisitations*, ed. Nadine Boehm-Schnitker and Susanne Gruss (London and New York: Routledge, 2014), 182.

25 Robin Gilmour, "Using the Victorians: the Victorian Age in Contemporary Fiction," in *Rereading Victorian Fiction*, ed. Alice Jekins and Juliet John (Houndmills: Palgrave Macmillan, 2002), 190.

26 Marie-Luise Kohlke, "Introduction: Speculations in and on the Neo-Victorian Encounter." *Neo-Victorian Studies* 1.1 (2008): 3.
27 Mitchell, *History and Cultural Memory in Neo-Victorian Fiction*, 1.
28 Kaplan, *Victoriana*, 5.
29 Heilmann and Llewellyn, *Neo-Victorianism*, 9.
30 Kohlke, "Introduction", 3.

1 Peter Ackroyd's Neo-Georgian Fiction

Reconstructing "the Age of Disguise"[1]

Jakub Lipski

Peter Ackroyd's (b. 1949) work has invariably manifested a reconciliation of novel writing with popular historiography and cultural studies, a trait that finds it fullest manifestation in the writer's unwavering interest in the form of the historical novel. Indeed, his literary output is a perfect illustration of a trend defined by George Rousseau as a "crossover of biography, history, and fiction", which, according to the critic, dominated the English literary scene in the three closing decades of the twentieth century.[2]

Among Ackroyd's numerous historical novels, there are three that reconstruct selected events of the Georgian period: *Hawksmoor* (1985), *Chatterton* (1987), *The Lambs of London* (2004).[3] These three works display similarities that suggest a coherent vision of the Georgian period, especially as they span almost the whole century. I would like to argue here that Ackroyd's choices of themes and (real-life) characters reconstruct the Georgian period as "the Age of Disguise", a concept put forward by Maximillian Novak in 1977.[4] Needless to say, I will not be trying to prove Ackroyd's direct indebtedness to Novak; rather a convergence of visions, the writer's implicit responsiveness to the way the Georgian period has been reconstructed and "post-modernised" in literary criticism since the 1970s and 1980s, when the first major studies of the eighteenth-century masquerade as a far-reaching socio-cultural practice, not just a form of entertainment, were published. The literary metaphor of disguise, as well as the related concepts of mask, theatre and performance, capture the essence of a time when the Delphic precept "know then thyself" acquired a new dimension. The first decades of the century brought about a lively philosophical debate over personal identity, now destabilised by the anti-substantialist approaches of John Locke and David Hume. At the same time, the masked assembly as a form of entertainment enjoyed a growing popularity, to the point where the metaphor of "world as masquerade" started to be used alongside the conventional *theatrum mundi* metaphor.[5] When seen in the context of each other, these two phenomena help to understand better the Georgian period and its typical socio-cultural conventions. The Polish critic Janusz Ryba goes as far as to talk about "Enlightenment masquerade-mania", and puts forward a very broad definition of the masquerade as "a rather extensive sphere of human gestures and behaviours, aiming at changing one's appearance or identity, pretending and misleading others by means of false 'creations'".[6] Ackroyd's use of thus broadly understood masquerade in his three neo-Georgian novels cannot surprise in the wider context of his work.

The metaphorical potential of disguise and masquerade is explored throughout Ackroyd's fiction. One of his earliest books, the 1979 piece of cultural history titled *Dressing Up, Transvestism and Drag: The History of an Obsession*, is often used as a context for the role of disguise and performance in Ackroyd's fictional works. For example, David Sexton goes as far as to call it "the key to all Peter Ackroyd's work".[7] I share this view, but it is worth noting that the book prioritises nineteenth-century material, especially late Victorian pantomime and the art of music halls. As this chapter will show, Ackroyd's neo-Georgian novels do the same cultural work as his neo-Victorian texts, thus providing a wider context for the recurring themes of the writer's output, and might even be read as a more profound reinterpretation of the historical moment.

Ackroyd's historical fiction should also be seen against the background of contemporaneous literary theories. The novelist began his writing career in the 1970s, when New Historicism problematised traditional ways of understanding history and historiography, pointing out their affinities with the genre of the historical novel. The concepts of masquerade, theatre and performance are then used as an interpretative prism through which Ackroyd revisions the Georgian period, very much in line with the fundamental assumption of new-historical studies that every historical writing is an individualised interpretative narrative. Importantly, this idea is also reflected at the intradiegetic level of the novels, with the protagonists both exploring the potential and struggling with the limits of historical reconstruction. Thus, Ackroyd's historical writing oscillates between two categories distinguished by Ansgar Nünning: *metahistorical fiction* and *historiographic metafiction*. The former, Nünning points out, features contemporary characters trying to reconstruct the past, thus putting emphasis on the nature of historical reconstruction itself – indicating its relativity, arbitrariness and inherent limits resulting from the fact that the process depends on a subjective interpretation of accessible sources.[8] *Historiographic metafiction* is a term that Nünning borrows from Linda Hutcheon's groundbreaking *A Poetics of Postmodernism* (1988). This type of fiction is also reflective of the postmodern trend to undermine positivist historiography by highlighting "epistemological problems attached to the mediation of historical events".[9] It foregrounds metafictionality by featuring a narrator or characters who explicitly ponder the nature of any textual mediation, including historiography. In Ackroyd's works, metafiction thus understood characterises both his third-person narrators and the characters struggling to reconstruct the past.

The Georgian period is then interpreted, rather than faithfully reconstructed, both by Ackroyd – the extra diegetic author – and by the characters within the fictional framework. My argument about the central role of the metaphor of disguise in the offered interpretation will be corroborated by the following readings of the plot, recurring images, motifs and themes, as well as the discourse of identity underpinning the narratives.

Stories of Frauds

The three novels tell stories of eighteenth-century frauds and forgers. The plots are convoluted, dissolving the binaries of past and present, as well as juxtaposing different historical moments. *Hawksmoor* offers two intertwined narratives: six odd-numbered chapters make up an archaically stylised first-person confession narrative of Nicholas Dyer, a fictional architect responsible for the realisation of a historical urban project in the years 1711–1715: the building of six Anglican churches meant to define the London cityscape after the fire of 1666. The six evenly-numbered chapters, in turn, constitute a modern crime story, featuring Detective Nicholas Hawksmoor trying to solve the case of mysterious murders uncannily connected with the six eighteenth-century churches. The two storylines permeate each other by way of troubling repetitions and structural parallels, thus creating an impression of circularity and atemporality. The interpretative possibilities of the novel have been largely explored in criticism, perhaps most fully by Susana Onega and David Malcolm,[10] so I will concentrate on the "masquerading" nature of Dyer's narrative.

The name itself is a mask, or "false creation", hiding the true name of the architect responsible for the six churches – Nicholas Hawksmoor (1661–1736), first an assistant to Sir Christopher Wren (who is also represented in Ackroyd's novel), and then an independent architect. The idea to use the real name for the contemporary detective, rather than the eighteenth-century architect, adds to the theme of uncanny doubling and serves as further complication to the temporal dimension of the narrative. Be that as it may, disguise is what already determines Dyer's narrative at this most basic level.

Hawksmoor-Dyer in Ackroyd's novel is a crypto-Satanist who uses church architecture as a vehicle for his occult messages. In Dyer's own words: "my Churches are the Vesture of other active Powers" (H, 180). The metaphor of vesture does not seem to be accidental here; rather, it situates Dyer's fraudulent design in the context of eighteenth-century masquerades, in particular, the so-called "architectural masquerades" as defined by Janusz Ryba. Writing about late eighteenth-century Poland, Ryba discusses the fashion for peasant cottages with lavish interiors among the nobility and relates it to the carnivalesque rituals at masked assemblies: aristocrats dressing up as peasants.[11] Even if Ryba analyses the phenomenon in the Polish context, it exemplifies a universal pattern of what might be termed antithetical masking; in *Hawksmoor*, this pattern underpins Dyer's idea to use sacred form to disguise diabolical content, while other popular manifestations of antithetical masking at eighteenth-century masquerades featured ladies of the night dressed up as nuns or clergymen as grotesque devils.

The narrative structure of *Chatterton* is even more complex, constituted, as it is, by three intertwined storylines taking place at three different historical moments: the story of Thomas Chatterton set forth in his first-person diary stylised in a manner reminiscent of Dyer's and in a third-person narrative from a twentieth-century perspective; the story of painter Henry Wallis (1830–1916), focusing on his work on the best-known painting representing dead Chatterton; finally, the twentieth-century story of Charles Wychwood, an unfulfilled poet in possession of hitherto unknown texts by Chatterton, who carries out his amateur investigation into the mysterious death of the eighteenth-century poet. These three levels are united not only by the figure of Chatterton but also by reflection upon art, creativity and originality provoked by the life of the famous forger.

Thomas Chatterton's (1752–1770) claim for fame was a series of forged publications that responded to the so-called Ossianic craze in the 1760s. Chatterton put on the mask of one Thomas Rowley, a fifteenth-century monk from Bristol, and specialised in narrative poems stylised as medieval ballads:

> I invented my self as a monk of the fifteenth century, Thomas Rowley; I dressed him in Raggs, I made him Blind and then I made him Sing. [...] Knowing my own Skill in the Art of Personation [...] I was a very Proteus to those who read my Works.
>
> (Ch, 87, 89)

Chatterton, however, had difficulty finding a publisher, and this, along with gradually more frequent accusations of forgery and critical voices, including such authorities as Horace Walpole, drove the young author to commit suicide, as was commonly believed. This, eventually, contributed to the formation of the myth of the doomed poet and gained Chatterton post-mortem fame among the Romantics and the Victorians.[12]

Chatterton's death is what unites the three narrative levels of Ackroyd's novel, which re-visions the event. The Henry Wallis story centres on his painterly representation of the poet's death – "The Death of Chatterton" (1856) – and his relationship with the model, the Victorian author George Meredith. The twentieth-century investigation into the death conducted by Charles Wychwood, in turn, ends with the amateur detective concluding that the suicidal death was a masquerade. The decisive piece of evidence is a newly found signed manuscript with a later date. Wychwood's documents also include Chatterton's poems and aphorisms, one of which is especially telling: "my Eyes are always upon thee, O lovely Delusion" (Ch, 60). After Wychwood's death, the investigation is continued by his friend Philip Slack, who finds out that Chatterton did commit suicide, and the newly discovered documents were forged by an eighteenth-century publisher. As if that were not enough, the third-person narrative to follow, possibly authored by Slack (who at one point ponders the idea of writing a novel about Chatterton), suggests that the death was an accident resulting from an unintentional overdose of arsenic and laudanum. This version has its supporters todays; it is offered as a "likely explanation" on the website of the Thomas Chatterton Society.[13]

The most recent of Ackroyd's neo-Georgian novels – *The Lambs of London* (2004) – shows a more unified narrative structure. It focuses on an episode in the lives of Charles Lamb (1775–1834), his sister Mary (1764–1847) and William Ireland (1775–1835), all important figures in the literary panorama of late-eighteenth-century London. Ackroyd returns to the theme of literary hoax and offers further reflection on the issues of authenticity and originality, which – after the success of *Chatterton* – appeared in some of his other novels as well (most notably, perhaps, in *Dan Leno and the Limehouse Golem* from 1994). Despite the title, the true protagonist of the novel is William Ireland.

Ireland's claim to fame were forged manuscripts of William Shakespeare. In 1794, he presented his father Samuel, a well-known travel writer of the time, with a legal document signed by Shakespeare. Once the authenticity of the signature was confirmed, Ireland proceeded to produce gradually more interesting pieces: a love letter to

Anne Hathaway (with a lock of Shakespeare's hair) and manuscripts of *Hamlet* and *King Lear*. The climactic point of his career as a hoax was the publication of the play *Vortigern* in 1795 and its premiere in Drury Lane Theatre orchestrated by Richard Sheridan, the most important personage in late eighteenth-century theatrical life. This, however, was too daring, and the play's strictly literary limitations resulted in Ireland's unmasking, authoritatively carried out by critic and Shakespearean researcher Edmund Malone in *An Inquiry into the Authenticity of Certain Miscellaneous Papers and Legal Instruments Attributed to Shakspeare* from 1796. It is worth noting that Malone relates Ireland's case to that of Thomas Chatterton, and in the novel the comparison is drawn by Ireland himself (LL, 71). In discussing Ireland's case, Malone resorts to what might be termed masquerade poetics: he writes about the "disguise of ancient spelling" and "clothing in old language".[14] Interestingly, if not confusingly, in Ackroyd's novel Malone is the one to first confirm the authenticity of Ireland's early documents.

Masquerade Poetics

Beyond the level of plot, Ackroyd's reconstruction of the Georgian period as "the Age of Disguise" depends on recurring themes, motifs and images that metaphorically create the atmosphere of an ongoing, never-ending masked ball or theatrical performance. Ackroyd, unsurprisingly, frequently resorts to the *theatrum mundi* topos and its narrower, typically eighteenth-century version – the topos of "the world as masquerade". At times this is only implied, like when Thomas de Quincey asks his friend Charles Lamb "Why must you see everything as drama, Charles?" (LL, 183). As a rule, however, these observations tend to be explicitly articulated: "the World being but a Masquerade, yet one in which the Characters do not know their Parts", reflects Nicholas Dyer (H, 173); "I am a strolling Player and this Chamber is my Theatre", writes the hoax masquerading as Thomas Chatterton (Ch, 86). Another topos that Ackroyd deploys is *fronti nulla fides* – place no trust on appearances – which does, of course, relate to the other two: in both *Hawksmor* and *Chatterton* the times are referred to as a "painted age" (H 175; Ch 89). Finally, both these novels repeatedly allude to the myth of Proteus, the shape-shifting sea god.

The same topoi and metaphors are used to characterise London. Admittedly, the central role of theatre, theatricality and performance for the image of the metropolis is an invariable characteristic throughout Ackroyd's fiction and non-fiction. In *London: The Biography*, the whole several-dozen-page-long section is devoted to the theatricality of London, with a very telling opening phrase "Show! Show! Show! Show! Show!" and a straightforward remark that "the theatricality of London is its single most important characteristic".[15] In his *Revolution*, the fourth volume of *The History of England* concerned with the long eighteenth century, Ackroyd calls Londoners "a society of the spectacle" and adds that in the eyes of contemporary novelists, the metropolis appears to be "a pantomime and a masquerade populated by grotesques".[16] In the same vein, in *London* Ackroyd invokes the words of Charles Lamb, who called the capital a "pantomime and masquerade",[17] while in *The Lambs of London* Charles describes the crowded streets of London as "a motley parade, part funeral procession and part pantomime" (LL, 27–28). To Nicholas Dyer, in turn, the city becomes a stage where the crowd puts on a show of their vices and degeneration (H, 94). In one of his interviews, Ackroyd openly remarked that to be a Londoner means to act: "they know they're living in a city in which they have to perform".[18]

The three neo-Georgian novels, as one would expect, feature several descriptions of theatrical performances and a number of references to masquerades, pantomimes and harlequinades taking place at the time. On the surface level, *The Lambs of London* is the novel that is the most preoccupied with theatre due to its subject matter: apart from the theatrical content, there are numerous allusions to Shakespeare and the ending may be read as a parody of the final scene in *A Midsummer Night's Dream*. Arguably, a more penetrating treatment of these forms of entertainment can be discerned from the two earlier novels. *Hawksmoor*, for example, offers an interesting blend of theatre and masquerade: Nicholas Dyer first sees a theatrical performance, then labels it a "masquerade" and leaves only to join a masked assembly in London. This juxtaposition implies an affinity between the two phenomena that explains the typically eighteenth-century concretisation of the world as theatre into the world as masquerade topos. In *Chatterton*, in turn, we read about the poet's fascination with a street posture master. Immediately before his death, Chatterton drinks to the street artist's health and calls him the "emblem of the world" (Ch, 223).

Finally, the three novels include mentions of masquerade schemes, defined as such on the linguistic level. To give two examples: in *Hawksmoor* we find such metaphorical expressions as "I hid my self with a woeful Countenance" (H, 25), while in *Chatterton* – "impersonate your own Fatality" (Ch, 92). This masquerade poetics is also complemented by secondary frauds (LL, 116), masked ladies of the night (H, 151), transvestites (H, 94), as well as mentions of such occupations as identity document forgery (Ch, 85–86).

Discourse of the Self

If the surface structure of Ackroyd's neo-Georgian fiction depends on a repetitive use of the discussed plot patterns, topoi, motifs and scenes, the deep structure is constituted by the offered discourse of the self. In this, Ackroyd addresses the core of the eighteenth-century obsession with masquerades – that is, the philosophical debate over the category of personal identity, most notably the ideas put forward by John Locke (identity as consciousness, not substance) and David Hume (identity as a theatre of fleeting ideas). Locke's and Hume's thought was also reworked by their contemporaries, who were able to offer more straightforward constructs of the self. For example, one Edmund Law, the Anglican bishop of Carlisle, published *A Defence of Mr. Locke's Opinion Concerning Personal Identity*, where he argued that the word "person" should be understood as

> a certain guise, character, quality, i.e. being in fact a mixed mode, or relation, and not a substance [...] it amounts to no more that saying, a man puts on a mask – continues to wear it for some time – puts off one mask and takes another.[19]

That said, Ackroyd's neo-Georgian novels do not explore eighteenth-century philosophies; rather, they ponder the category of the self with reference to twentieth-century thought, a strategy that accords not only with the general agenda behind neo-Georgian fiction, as is argued throughout this volume, but also with Ackroyd's own tendency to merge the different time levels. What underpins the vision of the Georgian period in the three novels is modern discourse of identity, in particular the theories of Sigmund Freud (*Doppelgänger*), Carl Gustav Jung (the Shadow archetype) and Jean Baudrillard (simulacrum). Admittedly, these concepts and their authors are not absent from the critical studies of the Georgian period that put an emphasis on the eighteenth-century masquerade. In *Masquerade and Civilization: The Carnivalesque in Eighteenth-Century English Culture and Fiction*, Terry Castle writes that the essence of masquerading should be understood in a Freudian manner – as ritualistic uncovering of the repressed,[20] which in turn relates to the theory of the double and the way it was reinterpreted by Jung. This Freudian dimension to masquerading would have been intuitively projected by the Georgians: Henry Fielding in his verse debut *The Masquerade* (1728) writes that the participants of a masked assembly "masque the face, t'unmasque the mind".[21] Baudrillard's notion of simulacrum has also been invoked in the context of eighteenth-century masquerades. Terry Castle, in *The*

Female Thermometer: Eighteenth-Century Culture and the Invention of the Uncanny, refers to it when writing about the illusive freedom and autonomy experienced by masqueraders,[22] while Nicholas Hudson, in a focused reading of *Tom Jones* by Henry Fielding, remarks that in a culture obsessed with masquerading, external determinants of social identity were mere "simulacrum of shirting surfaces".[23] Ping Wang has recently noted that masquerading does not necessarily imply hiding an identity; it may constitute a new reality where nothing is being hidden.[24] In a similar manner, Ronald L. Grimes writing on the phenomenology of masking argues that concealment is not the only mode of masking and distinguishes what he terms "masking as concretion", that is, "concretizing of dynamis in a fixed form".[25] Concretion as a mode of masking can be exemplified by those who cannot exist without their masks, just like the character-types of commedia dell'arte. These observations are surprisingly close to how Edmund Law defined personal identity almost three centuries before.

Coming back to Ackroyd's novels, the dominant aspect of the offered reflection upon personal identity is the *Doppelgänger*. It informs Ackroyd's discourse of the self in its two variants: doubling by way of similarity/repetition and doubling by way of contrast.[26] Structurally speaking, doubling is what organises Ackroyd's worlds in general – not only in terms of characterisation, but also in terms of plot, narrative, temporal dimensions and the relationship between the intradiegetic and extradiegetic levels. Nicholas Dyer is then an alter ego of the real Nicholas Hawksmoor, Chatterton a double of the fictitious Thomas Rowley and an alter ego of George Meredith, while William Ireland becomes a new incarnation of his famous namesake. As for the narrative structure, Ackroyd typically repeats the same images, scenes and events situating them in different temporal contexts. All this creates an impression of cyclicality and foregrounds the idea that history repeats itself, while also provoking reflection upon the (im)possibility of originality.

The motif of the double as contrast, the repressed uncovered, is most fully developed in *Hawksmoor*. It foregrounds the uncanny relationship between the architect Dyer-Hawksmoor with the contemporary detective Hawksmoor, who is in charge of the investigation into the series of murders somehow connected with the eighteenth-century churches designed by Dyer-Hawksmoor. In this, Ackroyd's novel follows the typical crime fiction convention of implied similarities between the investigator and the investigated.[27] In the eighteenth-century narrative itself, the patter of doubling by way of contrast juxtaposes Dyer and Christopher Wren. Contrasting a crypto-Satanist with an embodiment of Enlightenment harmony and rationalism in art is part of a larger plan; Susana Onega calls it an "all-encompassing duality" of rational empiricism and occult practices.[28] This vision of the Enlightenment corresponds to a general tendency of questioning the myth of a rational "Age of Reason" and discerning the tensions between the rational and the irrational that characterised this movement.[29] It is this critical tradition that gave way to a deepened reflection upon the masquerade as a socio-cultural phenomenon. That said, Dyer's character should not be limited to the role of rational Wren's repressed Shadow; rather, he illustrates the process of a gradual release of the repressed in the evolution of the self. To this end, the confessional narrative provides insight into Dyer's childhood and his transition towards darkness. It is not accidental, I would argue, that the word "shadow", sometimes spelled as "shaddow", recurs in the narrative with substantial frequency and is often used with a metaphorical dimension.

If split identity resulting from the release of the Shadow becomes a central aspect of *Hawksmoor's* discourse of the self, *Chatterton* and *The Lambs of London*, which both revolve around the question of inauthenticity, ponder the arbitrariness of the very notion of self, casting doubt on the belief in an authentic and unique "I". Both Chatterton and William Ireland create personae that are not constituted by any substantial personality. In Edmund Law's terms, their masks create a surface without any substance beneath; in Baudrillard's terms, their personae are copies without original referents. Indeed, as Samuel Ireland puts it, "origins are of no importance" (LL, 65). This is also implied in the conversation between Lamb's friends, as they are rehearsing one of the scenes of *A Midsummer Night's Dream*: " 'But they are characters. We are real. Aren't we?' / 'What does it signify, Ben? The words are the same, are they not?' " (LL, 90). The words are then autonomous and self-constitutive; the sign refers to itself without external referents. The idea that masks can live a life of their own, irrespective of the original, becomes a liberating thought for William Ireland. As he is watching a performance of the musical *Pizarro*, he thus expresses his admiration for the role of Charles Kemble:

> William watched Kemble with fascination. The man had become a Spanish general – not just in appearance and in manner, but in his being. He had become Pizarro, or had Pizarro become him? The breath of both had become one. William experienced a moment of elation. Here was proof that you might flee the prison of the self.
>
> (LL, 161)

In this utopian vision the disguise constitutes a new reality rather than hiding an original. In Baudrillard's words, "It is a question of substituting the signs of the real for the real".[30] This is exactly what Terry Castle wrote on the eighteenth-century masquerade, treating it as a utopian space of new liberated identities constituted by masks.

Chatterton shows a similar treatment of the metaphor of mask/ disguise. Let us recall that the posture master whom the protagonist admires is labelled "emblem of the world", and the postures adopted by the street artist illustrate the idea of the sign referring to itself. In a similar manner, the hoax depends for his identity on the meanings derived from the world of signs; there is no room for him in the world of external referents, no identity beyond the adopted mask. It is a condition that Baudrillard identifies as "pure simulacrum" – that is, the final stage in the process of representation separating itself from the represented.[31]

When in *Revolution* Ackroyd describes the incognito travel of Bonnie Prince Charlie to London in 1750, he writes: "He must have worn a mask and costume as he walked through the streets of London; but in that respect, he was very much part of a city that was often no more than a great stage".[32] This non-fiction history book does indeed offer further insight into the issues I have discussed here as the ideological core of Ackroyd's neo-Georgian fiction, with a separate chapter on the theatre and a number of catchphrases such as "the age of display" or "Everyone, from the politician to the preacher, took his cue from the stage";[33] nevertheless, one cannot help but gain the impression that the non-fictional reconstruction of the Georgian period in *Revolution*, perhaps unlike the one in *London*, places the emphasis elsewhere. To a large extent, the book is constituted by relatively traditional historiographic writing, with due attention given to the Grand History of politics, wars and commerce. The word "masquerade" is used once or twice, and there is literally no mention of masquerades as a form of mass entertainment. Why the change in perspective? One can only speculate, and if we follow up on the New Historicist assumption that historical fiction does not essentially differ from historiographic non-fiction, then we must accept the fact that the author is simply offering two different interpretations of the Georgian period. If, however, we return to appreciate the special role of the novel as a genre capturing the complexities of the self in the varying historical contexts and allowing for more narrative freedom, then the interpretations might be seen as complementary, and the one offered in the three novels, with their metahistorical (to invoke Ansgar Nünning typology) anachronistic lapses, micro-historical agenda and modern take on personal identity, might be indeed more successful in bringing the dialectics of the Georgian period closer to the here and now.

Notes

1 This chapter is a revised and updated version of an article I published in Polish: "'Wiek przebrania' w powieściach historycznych Petera Ackroyda", *Porównania. Czasopismo poświęcone zagadnieniom komparatystyki literackiej oraz studiom interdyscyplinarnym* 19 (2016), 99–113.

2 G.S. Rousseau, "Ingenious Pain: Fiction, History, Biography, and the Miraculous Eighteenth Century", *Eighteenth Century Life* 25 (2001), 48.

3 All the references to the three novels will be parenthetical and will use the following abbreviations: "H" for *Hawksmoor* (1985; Harmondsworth: Penguin Books, 1993); "Ch" for *Chatterton* (1987; Harmondsworth: Penguin Books, 1993); "LL" for *The Lambs of London* (2004; London: Vintage, 2005).

4 Maximillian E. Novak (ed.), *English Literature in the Age of Disguise* (Berkeley: University of California Press, 1977).

5 See Jakub Lipski, *In Quest of the Self: Masquerade and Travel in the Eighteenth-Century Novel. Fielding, Smollett, Sterne* (Amsterdam and New York: Rodopi, 2014), 21–34.

6 Janusz Ryba, *Maskarady oświeconych: Próba opisu zjawiska* (Katowice: Wydawnictwo Uniwersytetu Śląskiego, 1998), 19.

7 David Sexton, "Thereby hangs a tale. *Dan Leno and the Limehouse Golem* by Peter Ackroyd", *The Spectator* 8670 (1994), 33.

8 Christina Kotte, *Ethical Dimensions in British Historiographic Metafiction: Julian Barnes, Graham Swift, Penelope Lively* (Trier: WVT, 2001), 52.

9 Kotte, *Ethical Dimensions*, 54.

10 Susana Onega, *Metafiction and Myth in the Novels of Peter Ackroyd* (Columbia: Camden House, 1999), 43–92. David Malcolm, *Patterns and Literary Games in Peter Ackroyd's* Hawksmoor, *Interpretations of British Literature* 10 (Gdańsk: Wydawnictwo Gdańskie, 1995).

11 Janusz Ryba, *Oświeceniowe tutti frutti: Maskarady – konwersacja – literatura* (Katowice: Wydawnictwo Uniwersytetu Śląskiego, 2009), 36–37.

12 See Chapter 6 of Daniel Cook, *Thomas Chatterton and Neglected Genius, 1760-1830* (Houndmills: Palgrave Macmillan, 2013).

13 *Biography of Chatterton*, The Thomas Chatterton Society, www.thomaschattertonsociety.com/#!biography/cee5.

14 Edmund Malone, *An Inquiry into the Authenticity of Certain Miscellaneous Papers and Legal Instruments Attributed to Shakspeare* (1769; London: T. Cadell, Jun. and W. Davies, 1796), 32.

15 Peter Ackroyd, *London: The Biography* (2000; London: Vintage, 2001), 147, 152.

16 Peter Ackroyd, *The History of England. Volume IV: Revolution* (2016; London: Pan Books, 2017), 114, 189.

17 Ackroyd, *London*, 152. *London: The Biography* is a key to understanding Ackroyd's vision of London. Significantly, it foregrounds the characters and socio-cultural phenomena that feature in the neo-Georgian novels, and the categories of disguise, mask, masquerade and theatre are typically invoked to sketch a panorama of the Georgian period.

18 Jeremy Gibson and Julian Wolfreys, *Peter Ackroyd: The Ludic and Labyrinthine Text* (Houndmills: Palgrave Macmillan, 2000), 257.

19 Quoted after Dror Wahrman, *The Making of the Modern Self: Identity and Culture in Eighteenth-Century England* (New Haven Yale University Press, 2004), 196–197.

20 Terry Castle, *Masquerade and Civilization: The Carnivalesque in Eighteenth-Century English Culture and Fiction* (Stanford: Stanford University Press, 1986), 74.

21 Henry Fielding, *The Masquerade, A Poem Inscribed to C---T H--D--G--R* (London: J. Roberts, A. Dodd, 1728), 73–74.

22 Terry Castle, *The Female Thermometer: Eighteenth-Century Culture and the Invention of the Uncanny* (Oxford: Oxford University Press, 1995), 93.

23 Nicholas Hudson, "*Tom Jones*", in *The Cambridge Companion to Henry Fielding*, ed. Claude Rawson (Cambridge: Cambridge University Press, 2007), 81.

24 M. Kathryn Shields, "The Drama of Identity: Masking and Evolving Notions of Self in Contemporary Photography", in *Masquerade: Essays on Tradition and Innovation Worldwide*, ed. Deborah Bell (Jefferson: McFarland, 2015), 210.

25 Ronald L. Grimes, "Masking: Toward a Phenomenology of Exteriorization", *Journal of the American Academy of Religion* 43 (1975), 511.

26 For an insightful study on these two possibilities, see Gry Faurholt, "Self as Other: The Doppelgänger", *Double Dialogues* 10 (2009), www.doubledialogues.com/article/self-as-other-the-doppelganger.

27 David Malcolm studies the double motif with reference to the tradition of supernatural fiction. See Malcolm, *Peter Ackroyd's* Hawksmoor, 17–18.

28 Susana Onega, *Metafiction and Myth in the Novels of Peter Ackroyd* (Columbia: Camden House, 1999), 44.

29 See Malcolm, *Peter Ackroyd's* Hawksmoor, 40–44, for a discussion of how this conflicted view on the Age of Reason becomes a topic in the novel.

30 Jean Baudrillard, *Simulacra and Simulation*, trans. Sheila Faria Glaser (1981; Ann Arbor: University of Michigan Press, 2008), 2.

31 Baudrillard, *Simulacra and Simulation*, 6.

32 Ackroyd, *Revolution*, 143.

33 Ackroyd, *Revolution*, 111, 193.

2 Defoe's Foes

The Author As Character

Daniel Cook

Few Georgian authors have cameoed in works of fiction as often as Daniel Defoe has.[1] In his own lifetime he starred in Charles Gildon's satire *The Life and Strange Surprizing Adventures of Mr. D— De F—, of London, Hosier* (1719), soon after *Robinson Crusoe* was first published. The fictional cloning persists. Different Defoes appear prominently as spies-cum-authors in Diana Norman's *Shores of Darkness* (1996), Nicholas Griffin's *The House of Sight and Shadow* (2000) and Andrew Lane's *Dawn of Spies* (2016). Jake Arnott's Defoe is a seasoned story-fixer in *The Fatal Tree* (2017), where he and various hacks capture the confessions of convicted criminals. Harrumphing across the country alongside the modern-day narrator of Stuart Campbell's *Daniel Defoe's Railway Journey* (2017), a surreal iteration quite literally leaps out of the pages of a Penguin Classics edition of his real-life counterpart's travel writing. The most famous fictional Defoe features in J. M. Coetzee's *Foe* (1986), "a parable of canonical reading and rereading", as Radhika Jones puts it.[2] Reverting to one of his real names (Mr Foe), Defoe (Defawe, Faugh, Du Foo, Du' Foo, D'Foe, DeFoe, De Foe, or De Fooe[3]) is here a hired pen who conjures his best-known tale out of a memoir by a "true" castaway. That year, Defoe, a journalist, stole Robinson Crusoe's story in Gaston Compère's *Robinson '86*.[4] Setting aside a long train of neo-Georgian novels in which Defoe cameos as a seventeenth-century spy, a Defoe-as-character only for all intents and purposes, this chapter attends to two complex cases in the genre of author fictions: Coetzee's Foe and Campbell's Defoe.

Narrowing the focus will allow us to consider an array of tropes and techniques that trouble the seeming stability of author fictions as a bio-graphical genre. For Laura E. Savu the genre humanises familiar figures "in all their concrete particulars".[5] Within this purview these Defoes would be weak biofictional clones because they fail to conform to the concrete particulars of the flesh-and-blood man. A fantastical textual agent, Campbell's Defoe lacks stable corporeality as he simultaneously exhibits the signs of a mundane physicality (repeatedly touching his unsightly mole) and defies the laws of physics (hiding and residing in a book at will). Although confined to a modern copy of *A Tour through the Whole Island of Great Britain*, he speaks in repurposed fragments from a range of already published works, and even offers new observations in response to present stimuli. Coetzee's Foe, more than thirty years earlier, had left behind traces of a bodily existence, in the tatty clothes, wigs, papers and pens strewn across his barely furnished writing room.[6] If, as Patrick Corcoran puts it, Foe is "the writer who is reluctant to write",[7] Campbell's Defoe is the writer who cannot stop. Both caricature their real-life peer's marketplace machinations: scribbling for survival. Read as metafictional commentary, Coetzee's 1986 novel belongs in the tradition set by Gildon's 1719 *Life*, where Defoe's characters lay claim to an independent existence in threatening to punish the author "for making us such Scoundrels in thy Writing".[8] Foe is wholly dependent on other characters – not merely for the books he produces but for the very existence he has within the neo-Georgian text. Like Campbell's Defoe, Foe should be considered as a character-like author and as an author-like character, rather than a poststructuralist conflation of the roles. By character-like I mean to suggest that the figures recall but do not embody the real Defoe or the connotations with which his name has become associated. Author-like denotes a knowingly pantomimic existence in the service of narrative rather than an otherwise blandly biofictional personation of "the author".

Tellingly, other characters in each novel take on the dual roles of author and narrator most of the time. Susan Barton, in *Foe*, reluctantly picks up the pen literally and figuratively abandoned by the eponymous figure. A writer in his own right, the unnamed narrator of *Daniel Defoe's Railway Journey* contends with a scribbling ghost who refuses to be shut away. As a character, Foe is written into existence by Susan, an amateur memoirist keenly conscious of her pre-novel experiences, as she needs a noteworthy hack to superintend her materials into print. Eventually, Susan realises that Foe the author has written her into existence. Cruso (a fuzzy version of Crusoe), meanwhile, has little interest in recounting his version of the shipwreck story, so Coetzee swiftly kills him off. A tongueless Friday has had his voice taken away. In his more recent novel, Campbell provides a similarly counterintuitive exemplar of the author-as-character topos: his Defoe, though faithfully carried around in a dog-eared paperback, is frequently shut away, interrupted or otherwise rendered mute by the exacerbated narrator whenever he seeks to record new experiences and thereby write himself back into existence. These Defoes riff on the paradigm of the professional author who has accrued (or is perpetually accruing) a recognisable if restless body of works. Coetzee and Campbell work with and against Defoe, the author-as-character and (within the texts) the character-as-author.

Coetzee's Foe; or, Who Is the Author?

"My novel, *Foe*, if it is about any single subject", Coetzee writes, "is about authorship: about what it means to be an author in the professional sense [...] The notion that one can be an author as one can be a baker is fairly fundamental to my conception of *Foe*".[9] Foe has not yet written *Robinson Crusoe* or *Roxana*, but he has already produced a short anecdote attributed to the flesh-and-blood Defoe, *The Apparition of Mrs Veal*, a copy of which Susan Barton uses as proof of his credentials:

> "This is a book, Friday," I say. "In it is a story written by the renowned Mr Foe. You do not know the gentleman, but at this very moment he is engaged in writing another story, which is your story, and your master's, and mine".[10]

Frustrated with the absconded author, Susan later defines him as a hired pen adept at "writing up" with little apparent invention the stories of "those thieves or highwaymen of yours who gabble a confession and are then whipped off to Tyburn and eternal silence" (123). By that point, Susan has grown uneasy with scribal authorship as she realises that its apparent artlessness obfuscates its unvetted fabrication, "leaving you to make of their stories whatever you fancy" (123). This Foe will fix the materials sent to him just as casually as a tailor alters clothes.

For Jean-Paul Engélibert, taking the connection between Foe and Defoe too literally, the persona of the author-as-character "does not serve as a way of fixing the origins of the text, but on the contrary of showing the impossibility of writing about origins".[11] Dominic Head, furthermore, suggests that Foe the author caricatures poststructuralism as "a cavil over words", a "dispute we know to be endless".[12] But origin is just one facet of a complex matrix of authorial concerns in *Foe*, in which the mechanics of writing itself are just as prominent. And the book has multiple text-bounded endings. After all, we begin the book with a finished product, a completed memoir by Susan Barton. Later, in her pursuit of Foe, we learn that her own memoir (the pre-text, as it were) had taken her barely three days of cramped composition in bed (61). Foe never completes his reworking (a novelisation of the memoir), though in conversation with Susan he does outline its structure. Against that unwritten (or pre-written) book, *Foe* is itself structured in four main parts, setting aside the sectional breaks indicated by asterisks. The first part, we belatedly learn, comprises the lost shipwreck memoir upon which Foe is tasked with basing his ghost-written book for Susan.

Softly mimicking eighteenth-century typographical practice, each paragraph of Susan's story has been enclosed in inverted commas. As persistent markers on the page, the inverted commas signal Susan's ownership of the story; equally they mark it off as enclosable, quotable, and therefore extractable. Susan, in this part, continually emphasises the tension between authorship and ownership. Early on, for instance, she tells her audience (Foe, we soon learn) about how she met Cruso (the logophobic counterpoint to Defoe's Crusoe):

> I would gladly recount to you the history of this singular Cruso, as I heard it from his own lips. But the stories he told me were so various, and so hard to reconcile one with another, that I was more and more driven to conclude age and isolation had taken their toll on his memory, and he no longer knew for sure what was truth, what fancy.
>
> (11–12)

Cruso is an anti-author, or at least an anti-Crusoe who "kept no journal, perhaps because he lacked paper and ink, but more likely, I now believe, because he lacked the inclination to keep one, or, if he ever possessed the inclination, had lost it" (16). Writing in the first-person voice, Defoe's eponymous narrator performs the labour of writing in *Robinson Crusoe*: "now it was when I began to keep a Journal of every Day's Employment".[13] Cruso's lack of record-keeping perturbs Susan: "would you not wish for a memorial to be left behind, so that the next voyagers to make landfall here, whoever they may be, may read and learn about us, and perhaps shed a tear?" (17). This speech conflates seemingly incompatible notions of authorship. The first is a hermeneutic model of authorship in which Susan intends to record their lives as accurately as possible.[14] The second is a novelistic model predicated on human interest, which would fit with the pseudo-autobiographical approach taken in Defoe's fictions. A significant difference concerns their approach to the materials. Susan wants a complete account; Crusoe favours highlights that expend "many dull things".[15] Crusoe pre-exists his book ("I was born in the Year 1632, in the City of York, of a good family...").[16] But Coetzee's Foe has been brought into being, as Alexandra Effe puts it, by Susan, solely to record her story and therefore bring her to life.[17]

Postmodern authors, for Brian McHale, are at once vehicles of auto-biographical fact within the projected fictional world and the maker of that world.[18] Foe is a co-opted conjurer. Susan's authorship entails recording rather than creating, whatever writerly tools may be lying around: "to burn the story upon wood, or engrave it upon rock?" (17). Cruso implicitly follows a similar model of authorship, one thwarted by circumstance. As Friday's tongue has been cut out, he will never be able to tell his story: "How will we ever know the truth?", Cruso laments (23).[19] Does such limitation suggest a lack of imagination or an over-zealous commitment to the story? In any case, Susan is aware that the reader "expects stories from its adventurers" (34). Cruso is neither a storyteller nor an adventurer. Read within a metafictional purview, the conversation Susan has with Captain Smith, to whom she told "my story, as I have told it to you" (40), takes on extra importance. Unlike Cruso, the captain encourages the author: " 'It is a story you should set down in writing and offer to the booksellers', he urged – 'There has never before, to my know-ledge, been a female castaway of our nation. It will cause a great stir' ". Despondent, Susan shakes her head. "A liveliness is lost in the writing down which must be supplied by art", she concedes, "and I have no art". Captain Smith retorts that "the booksellers will hire a man to set your story to rights, and put in a dash of colour too, here and there". (Built into this account of Georgian bookselling practices is an assumption that a male author will need to enhance the female castaway's story.)

Susan, disagreeing, reasserts her hermeneutic principles: "their trade is in books, not in truth". "If I cannot come forward, as author, and swear to the truth of my tale, what will be the worth of it?" (40). Inadvertent or otherwise, the pun on *worth* (ethically, monetarily) signals again the tension between authorship and ownership that troubles Susan and, as we shall see, drives Foe. Here, Foe more closely resembles Defoe – or rather, Coetzee-the-critic's account of Defoe as "a businessman trading in words and ideas", not an artist.[20] The opening part of *Foe* ends with a direct address to the professional author to whom Susan will entrust her story:

> Do you think of me, Mr Foe, as Mrs Cruso or as a bold adven-turess? Think what you may, it was I who shared Cruso's bed and closed Cruso's eyes, as it is I who have disposal of all that Cruso leaves behind, which is the story of his island.
>
> (45)

The first question gestures towards a crisis of characterisation seen in Gildon's metafictional *Life* as early as 1719: will Foe make her a diminished figure in Cruso's shipwreck memoir or will he promote her above a man whom Susan earlier characterised as a reluctant story-teller, and ergo a failed adventurer? Whether sharing Cruso's bed, as a pretended wife who calls herself Mrs Cruso solely to mitigate gossip, or closing the corpse's eyes after his death on board Captain Smith's ship, Susan presents herself as the shaper of the story's raw material. If not quite an author – not yet – she remains an owner.

Dear Mr Foe

Foe rejects the story he receives on behalf of a prospective readership with little interest in truth, as Annamaria Carusi argues.[21] In Macaskill and Colleran's reading, the exchange between the female castaway and her appointed scribe amounts to a grotesque form of collaboration that extends beyond "a competitive literary labouring to become a working on behalf of the enemy, a siding with the foe".[22] Lewis MacLeod offers a different reading: Susan "hasn't been hijacked by narrative conscription so much as she has been outplayed in a game she volunteers to play".[23] Foe says as much (presumably in Susan's paraphrasing, the quotation marks notwithstanding): "I did not ask you to come visiting, you came of your own will" (120). I propose an alternative view: Susan's Foe is not a biofictional Defoe but rather a Defoevian character-as-author. Defoe's narrators assert their autonomy. In *Serious Reflections During the Life and Surprising Adventures of Robinson Crusoe* (1720), Defoe (in character as Crusoe) insists that "there's not a Circumstance in the imaginary Story, but has its just Allusion to a real Story, and chimes Part for Part, and Step for Step with the inimitable Life of *Robinson Crusoe*".[24] On behalf of the title character, the fictional editor of *Roxana* similarly asserts the uniqueness of the story: "*this* Story *differs from most of the Modern Performances of this Kind* [...] *the Foundation of This is laid in Truth of* Fact".[25] Susan begs Foe to take her unique story ("You have not heard a story before like mine"), wilfully monetising her value ("I am the good fortune we are always hoping for", 48). (Missing the mercantile pun on "good fortune", Judie Newman assumes Susan presents herself "innocently" as a figure of fortune in need of rescue.[26]) Foe does not respond, but he does invest in her: he gives her three guineas and lodging, so we learn in a follow-up letter from Susan. In material terms, Susan will have no financial independence until her book (a novelisation of her memoirs) hits the market. "Will you not bear it in mind", she reminds Foe, "that my life is drearily suspended till your writing is done?" (63).

Despite her reservations about scribal authorship, Susan must take up the pen of the absent author when she finds herself in his barely furnished room: "I have your table to sit at, your window to gaze through. I write with your pen on your paper, and when the sheets are completed they go into your chest. So your life continues to be lived, though you are gone" (65). For Susan, writing is an assertion of authority, even if the game of bookselling excludes her. The act of writing, in other words, offers bodily autonomy:

> I sat at your bureau this morning [...] and took out a clean sheet of paper and dipped pen in ink – your pen, your ink, I know, but somehow the pen becomes mine while I write with it, as though growing out of my hand.
>
> (66–67)

Though she may not realise it, this uncanny bodiliness matches Defoe's Roxana, a character tacitly based on Foe's Susan after the fact: Roxana will "give my own Character [...] as if I was speaking of another-body".[27] As she gains confidence, Susan moves away from the hermeneutic model of authorship towards novelistic invention: "Are these enough strange circumstances to make a story of?" (67). She even second-guesses Foe's market-led alterations: you will say to yourself "Better without the woman" (72). Ironically, she is right – Foe's real-life alter ego relocates Susan to another novel, *Roxana*. To her dismay, Susan gradually recognises that Foe's powers of invention are so potent he can conjure up flesh-and-blood characters, such as a "father-born" child claiming to be Susan's daughter, with whom she shares her full name (Susan Barton).

Favouring realism in fiction, Susan (the putative biological mother) considers the invention of the child to be absurd as it lacks generic precedent: "The world is full of stories of mothers searching for sons and daughters they gave away once, long ago. But there are no stories of daughters searching for mothers" (77). This is not the first time the sly inventiveness of Defoe-as-author has angered his creations. In one of the most surreal scenes in Gildon's 1719 *Life*, Defoe's characters wreak savage revenge on the writer by making him eat a copy of the book in two volumes: "me will make him swallow his own Vomit", Friday warns.[28] Largely an homage to the real Defoe, Jane Gardam's *Crusoe's Daughter* (1985) ends with an elderly Polly Flint conversing with a shadowy figure identified as Crusoe, with whom she discusses the fictionality of *Robinson Crusoe*. "My creator had quite a facility", claims Crusoe, conceding authority to the author; "Stood him in very good stead. Memoirs". "Nonsense", retorts Polly, "he made it all up".[29] Susan herself has been conjured up by Foe, so she slowly apprehends. Inadvertently, she had raised that possibility in our minds, as eaves-dropping readers, when she calls herself "a being without substance, a ghost beside the true body of Cruso", and implores Foe to return "to me the substance I have lost" by telling her story (51).[30] At the outset, Susan had sought out Foe because of his reputation as a writer-up of sources, such as *The Apparition of Mrs Veal*, and not as a novelist prone to market-led invention.

When confronted later, Foe outlines his conjuring model of author-ship in rather explicit terms: "In a life of writing books, I have often, believe me, been lost in the maze of doubting" (135). The trick to authorial conjuring, as Foe puts it, is "to plant a sign or marker in the ground where I stand" (135–136). If, as Susan Naramore Maher suggests, Susan is "a conglomerate of novelistic conventions", she is precisely the sort of marker upon which an experienced writer such as Foe would rely.[31] Another character seemingly lifted from Defoe's *Colonel Jack* makes an appearance: Jack, "a notable pick-pocket" (128). As with Susan and her alleged daughter, Foe refuses to take responsi-bility for Jack ("[he] has his own life to live", 128). In this reading, Susan is a reluctant author who abandons her property; Foe is an opportun-istic writer who manipulates whatever he finds. Defoe's Jack the pick-pocket has been quietly repurposed by Foe as Jack the messenger boy. If Foe represents (to Susan's mind) the quintessential eighteenth-century author who gains professional status only when reworking found materials, Susan is more like the postmodernist author who, in Brian McHale's words, flickers in and out of existence. "I continued to trust in my own authorship", she asserts. Yet within a matter of lines she becomes "doubt itself": "Who is speaking me? Am I a phantom too?" (133). Even when lost in a maze of doubting, Foe never loses his crafts-manship. We finally meet him, substantially at least, in the third part of the novel, which switches to first-person narration with reported speech (as opposed to an authored memoir or one-way epistolary exchange).

Susan and Friday find Foe in Bristol. Some basic hospitality aside, Foe promptly resumes the role of the professional author. He does not write, in the mechanical sense, as Susan does. But he gathers his sources, and composes his structure, out loud. Against Susan's indeterminacy, Foe summarises the gist of the story he wishes to write up:

> We therefore have five parts in all: the loss of the daughter; the quest for the daughter in Brazil; abandonment of the quest, and the adventure of the island; assumption of the quest by the daughter;

and reunion of the daughter with her mother. It is thus that we make up a book: loss, then quest, then recovery; beginning, then middle, then end. As to novelty, this is lent by the island episode – which is properly the second part of the middle – and by the reversal in which the daughter takes up the quest abandoned by her mother.

(117)

Susan does not wish to shape the story in such a way: "All the joy I had felt in finding my way to Foe", she says to herself, "fled me". But the island story is nothing more than a loaf of bread, Foe reasons: "It will keep us alive, certainly, if we are starved of reading; but who will prefer it when there are tastier confections and pasties to be had?" However, Susan later reaffirms her longstanding faith in a hermeneutic model of authorship: "These I would not accept because they were not the truth" (121). She also more boldly asserts her authorial rights: "It is still in my power to guide and amend"; "Above all, to withhold". She will be "father to my story" (123). Foe attempts to nullify Susan's newfound desire to father her own story by conjuring up two anecdotes in which he asserts the power of his authorship. One is the confession of an Irishwoman sentenced to death for committing infanticide and bigamy, among other things. The moral of the story, claims Foe, is to recognise the importance of telling your story but then holding your peace for ever after. Susan, more cynically, suggests instead that the moral is: be wary of the appointed author who gets the final word.

Foe's second anecdote concerns a condemned woman worried about the infant daughter she will leave behind. A gaoler and his wife finally agree to adopt the child. The application, says Foe, is that there are "more ways than one of living eternally" (125). Entrusting her child to strangers, like Susan trusting her story to Foe, the nameless woman can rest easy. In retaliation, Susan conjures up her own authorial motif, lamenting that there is no such thing as a "man-Muse, a youthful god who visited authoresses in the night and made their pens flow" (126). The insinuation of reproductive fertility circles back to the borrowed paternalism innate to Susan's hermeneutic model. Where Foe's authorial parables casually reinscribe a singular flow of materials, from the female body to the male pen, Susan favours an image of sexual power verging on violence: "It is always a hard ride when the Muse pays her visits" (140). She also makes a telling quip about being paid for sex that revisits her ongoing concerns about the vexed relation-ship between authorship and ownership: "he gave me sixpence, which, though no great payment for a visit from the Muse, I accepted" (145). Money aside, this bodily interaction between the male author and the female subject suggests a collaboration between muse and author will always be vital for productivity: "She must do whatever lies in her power to father her offspring" (140). The gender confusion here (fathering her offspring) continues in her challenge to his professionalism: "Am I to damn you as a whore for welcoming me and embracing me and receiving my story?" (152). Ultimately, she embraces Foe's model of appropriation by shifting the value judgements: "It is not whoring to entertain other people's stories and return them to the world better dressed", she informs him (151–152).

Foe ends with a curious coda, or a reboot, as Jo Alyson Parker has it.[32] An unknown narrator – a new author of sorts – surveys a dusty room three hundred years after the events of the main part of the novel have occurred. The lifeless bodies of the characters lay strewn on the floor, their skin "dry as paper" (153). Foe's name is restored; or perhaps a separate Defoe has been referenced: "At one corner of the house, above head-height, a plaque is bolted to the wall. *Daniel Defoe, Author*, are the words, white on blue, and then more writing too small to read" (155). The memorialising model of authorship that Susan had largely championed, before she adopted the role of Defoevian scribbler, gives way to a more literal memorialisation of the real-life author. At the same time, Susan's pre-text memoir, the bulk of part one of *Foe*, remains. The reboot does not threaten to "unwrite" the story, as Tisha Turk would have it.[33] After all, we even return to the first line: "Bringing the candle nearer, I read the first words of the tall, looping script: 'Dear Mr Foe, At last I could row no further'" (155). In fact, a slight discrepancy occurs between the lines. Only here, at the end, do we have the address to "Dear Mr Foe". To whom does the story really belong, then? Who has the final word? Which authorial model finally triumphs? Where is Defoe, really?

Travels with Defoe

Introducing him as the canonical author of *Robinson Crusoe* and *Moll Flanders*, *Daniel Defoe's Railway Journey* reminds readers that Defoe also published *A Tour through the Whole Island of Great Britain*. The publisher even provides an approximate facsimile of the original title page for the latter, a suitably bookish relic in a metafictional novel. Along with another eccentric pensioner (as the book's blurb styles them), named John, the unnamed narrator undertakes a series of long-distance train journeys with "one of my literary heroes, Daniel Defoe".[34] Unlike the jobbing Foe, this fictive clone has lived his life. Now he is a textual ghost conjured out of the pages of a Penguin Classics edition.

Hero worship notwithstanding, Stuart Campbell draws the eponymous character in markedly different shades: as petty, puritanical, flirtatious, sombre, and sarcastic, among other things. This Defoe is a product of his period ("as a protestant dissenter you have strong opinions on these matters", the narrator tells him, "but frankly, I don't want to hear them", 21). Equally, he remains alert to modern concerns ("The miners have my sympathy", he observes in passing, 55). (Foe, by contrast, outsources the faculty of observation to Susan: "Come back and report to me how the world does" (*Foe*, 150)). Positioned within the genre of author fictions, Campbell's Defoe recalls the historical figure Daniel Defoe expressly as a canonical author. But, read in a metafictional context alongside the more sardonic *Foe*, the book-dwelling genie is better understood as a textual gimmick through which Campbell explores the comical mundanity of the experiences shared by jobbing writers across the ages.

The narrator will embrace "embellishment" (his word) as a universally human instinct that, so he claims with knowing irony, is decidedly not "a disingenuous literary ploy" (xv). Unlike Coetzee's Susan, the narrator more matter-of-factly adopts the habits of a Defoevian author (by his definition): "Who would I accost? Whose stories would I steal?" (43). As a professional author, Campbell's Defoe follows two impulses: an intellectual need to record his observations about the world around him and a perpetual fear of debt. Coetzee's Foe has a similar fear, perhaps more overwhelmingly so, as his writerly impulse gets subsumed into hack work. Although singled out for his renown among hired pens, Foe has not yet written the fictional masterpieces with which Coetzee's novel most blatantly engages, *Robinson Crusoe* and *Roxana*. Not only has Campbell's Defoe written *A Tour*, by contrast, his book has long been a "classic". That said, the modern narrator does not statically canonise the work so much as engage with its author's restless spirit: "Although he seemed quite contained within the 700-odd pages of my well-thumbed Penguin Classic, there was no guarantee that a spirit so passionate, curious and contradictory would be happy to stay there for long" (xvi). The author-as-character in Coetzee's novel might be called a parallel Defoe, one that has yet to write his major works of fiction. In Campbell's, he has been boxed into a single-volume construct, even if he is also more akin to a conventional fictional character capable of demonstrating independent agency.

A sign of the restraints imposed on his character comes early on, when the narrator notices that his companion looks anxious: "The cockiness he had shown just moments earlier had vanished" (14). "I remembered a reference in his biography to moments of black despair when hounded by creditors", the narrator continues. Coetzee teasingly conflates Foe with the works of his flesh-and-blood counterpart, as well as the authorial personae associated with those works; this Defoe, in a different way, cannot escape the historical circumstances defined by his real-life self's autobiographical (and biofictional) records. The author-as-character in *Daniel Defoe's Railway Journey* cannot straight-forwardly be called a fictive clone of Defoe. He is a fantastical representative of the imperilled authors who strove for recognition in the age of anonymous print: "A writer's lot is a thankless task", the made-up Defoe observes; "You could end up impoverished and imprisoned" (134). At the same time, Campbell's Defoe conforms to the paradigm of the successful, "classical" author at once subjected to the haphazard machinations of the marketplace ("Printers! Pah! The spawn of the devil. They'll pirate your work for a shilling") and given a catalogable name, an authorial brand ("Now it is written by Daniel Defoe", 247). Regardless, this Defoe keeps writing throughout his journeys: "Defoe [...] put aside the manuscript he was working on, shook his head and sighed" (65). A bookish afterlife prolongs his writerly impulses even as it frustrates them.

Campbell's Defoe certainly takes the profession of authorship very seriously. He frequently attacks the narrator for his comparative shortcomings: " 'Do your duty', said Defoe who was becoming annoyed at my apparent reluctance to talk to other passengers" (33). And he asserts his own expertise: "I speak with authority. I wrote a History of the Devil" (105). But he is also restrained by his pre-established author-ship. Although he freely walks out and about in the streets with the narrator, Campbell's Defoe, as a textual figment of the imagination, remains largely tethered to his papery cage. "Back into your book!", the narrator blasts at him (21). Defoe's introduction within the novel is absurd: "Without warning, Defoe burst from page 576! The cloying reek of civet from his perfumed wig filled the carriage" (2). The account evokes a human body, but only by association (smells, chiefly). Belatedly, almost fifty pages later, the narrator does describe Defoe's appearance in the terms we would expect with any regular character:

Defoe was asleep and I took the opportunity to stare at him.

"A middle siz'd spare man, about forty years old, of a brown complexion, and dark brown-coloured hair, but wears a wig; a hooked nose, a sharp chin, grey eyes and a large mole near his mouth."

He opened his eyes, he had obviously heard every word.

"How dare you!"

"Sorry?"

"You stole those words from the *London Gazette*. If you recall, they were prefaced with the invocation, 'Whosoever shall discover Defoe so he may be apprehended...' And all because of a piddling pamphlet that I penned in an idle moment."

(51)

An extreme textuality unsettles a seemingly straightforward description. The description, that is, has been borrowed (as Defoe recognises) from a contemporary periodical. As an historical figure – and a familiar author, no less – Defoe has become a repository of lived experiences ("That lawyer! He's pursuing me for the debts I can't pay", 194). At the same time, as a character who can continue to express opinions, he will not be a closed book: "'One of my children died when I was in Newgate prison', said Defoe, who had been surprisingly quiet up until this point. When the time was right I would probe him about his incarceration, but now wasn't the time" (39).

As a repository of knowledge who jumps out of his book when summoned, a papery genie rather than a verbal simulacrum of a human being, he is subject to a reader's spontaneous inquiry: "Realising that part of me was actually missing him", the narrator writes, "I held *A Tour through the Whole Island* by the front and back covers and shook it, but he wasn't for coming out" (82–83). On other occasions, the narrator-as-reader craves peace from his imaginary companion: "Mercifully, Defoe crept back into the book and pulled the pages over his head" (16). At other times, the narrator chastises Defoe: "'Stop right there'. He looked up, confused. 'If I remember, you spend the next twenty odd pages describing the building in tedious detail'" (86). And, offsetting the apparent hero worship of the elder author, the narrator frequently becomes overfamiliar: "Do you really think so, Danny? Surely a small hint of hyperbole there? We have had this discussion before" (237). The narrator does not wish to provoke his "imaginary friend", to be sure, but their exchanges can be competitive when it comes to their role and function as authors. More than that, the narrator hints at a discord between them: "This was a good conversation, only spoiled by Defoe's intrusion" (92). Later, he even asserts complete control: "I wasn't certain that I had granted Defoe permission to instigate conversations. He was my creature, and accordingly could only respond when I chose" (159). The fictional author – the Great Fabricator, as Pat Rogers dubs him in the Penguin Books edition[35] referenced by Campbell – goads the narrator:

> "Look", I said. "Sometimes I make things up. I mix fact with invented nonsense."
>
> "The delineation between what is observable and the fruits of your odd imagination should be clearer."
>
> "Look, whose book is this?"
>
> "I suggest Sir, you look again at the title that you have chosen for your narrative." He smiled smugly.
>
> (28)

Much later, the narrator finds a definitive way of dealing with the fictional agitator: "I snapped shut my Penguin Classic, cutting him off in mid-sentence" (192). Interrupted or suspended sentences recur throughout the book, though with less overt violence than in the writerly exchanges between Susan and Foe in Coetzee's 1986 novel: "Defoe also did his best to encourage me but to little effect. He even offered to take over the narrative but he too struggled to find much to say" (268). And when Campbell's narrator appropriates the words of the real Defoe he puts them into quotation marks and gives them to the author's biofictional peer. Even then, polite citation can be immediately undermined by an in-text reaction: "I think we know that, Daniel", the narrator quips (273). Nevertheless, the pertinent point here is this: even when appropriating Defoe, Campbell retains the authorial integrity of the original. If anything, he enhances the authorial integrity of the original as the words he quotes in *Daniel Defoe's Railway Journey* largely come from belatedly attributed works. An abrupt death of sorts comically undercuts the narrator's bantering veneration for Defoe:

> On the train back to Glasgow I asked John if my copy of *The Tour* had fallen off his side of the table.
>
> "Christ!" he said. "It must have been with the papers when the man came collecting rubbish."
>
> "What!" I said.
>
> "I must have bundled everything up together."
>
> I felt a profound sense of loss. It was only a paperback but I was bereft. My Figment had left me.
>
> (317)

The inky legacy of the once-flesh-and-blood author Defoe will survive, even if the semi-sentient Defoe of this novel has been farcically snuffed out. A death of a copy – a literal copy of the book, as it were – nevertheless causes some distress for the human companion who conjured the make-believe Defoe into being. Characters die in books only until readers bring them back to life again. But the loss of a book remains permanent, unless the reader can procure another copy.

The author-as-character explicitly named as Defoe (or Foe) in contemporary author fictions resembles in appearance (however unreliably) and (in parts) the seventeenth-century figure we now call Daniel Defoe. In *Daniel Defoe's Railway Journey* he becomes a bookish genie flitting in and out of a Penguin Classics edition of one of his lesser known works. In *Foe* he is a largely absent scribbler renowned for fixing stories such as Susan Barton's "true" tale of the female castaway. The metafictional games extend into other novels that lie beyond our scope here. Jake Arnott's Defoe in *The Fatal Tree* similarly reworks raw materials into literature, though primarily he is an important spy. A spymaster in Andrew Lane's "Crusoe Adventure" series, Diana Norman's *Shores of Darkness*, and Nicholas Griffin's *The House of Sight and Shadow*, among other recent works, Daniel Defoe habitually occupies the imaginative pockets between truth and fiction. The Great Fabricator has himself been refabricated again and again, against his will or otherwise.

Notes

1 For a representative list of authors as characters see *Biographical Fiction: A Reader*, ed. Michael Lackey (London and New York: Bloomsbury, 2017), 427–436. See also *The Author as Character: Representing Historical Writers in Western Literature*, ed. Paul Franssen and Ton Hoenselaars (London: Associated University Presses, 1999).

2 Radhika Jones, "Father-Born: Mediating the Classics in J. M. Coetzee's *Foe*", *Digital Defoe* 1.1 (2009), 47. See also Linda Carter, "Contaminated Copies: J. M. Coetzee's *Foe*", in *Generic Instability and Identity in the Contemporary Novel*, ed. Madelena Gonzalez and Marie-Odile Pittin-Hédon (Newcastle: Cambridge Scholars Publishing, 2010), 26–33, and Derek Attridge, "Oppressive Silence: J. M. Coetzee's *Foe* and the Politics of Canonisation", in *Critical Perspectives on J. M. Coetzee*, ed. Graham Huggan and Stephen Watson (Basingstoke and London: Macmillan, 1996), 168–190.

3 See John Robert Moore, *Daniel Defoe: Citizen of the Modern World* (Chicago: University of Chicago Press, 1958), 7–8.

4 For *Robinson '86* see Jean-Paul Engélibert, "Daniel Defoe as Character: Subversion of the Myths of Robinson Crusoe and of the Author", in *Robinson Crusoe: Myths and Metamorphoses*, ed. Lieve Spaas and Brian Stimpson (London: Macmillan; New York: St Martin's, 1996), 267–281.

5   Laura E. Savu, *Postmortem Postmodernists: The Afterlife of the Author in Recent Narrative* (Madison NJ: Fairleigh Dickinson Press, 2009), 15. See also Aleid Fokkema, "The Author: Postmodernism's Stock Character", in *The Author as Character*, ed. Franssen and Hoenselaars, 39–51.

6   On Defoe's and Foe's divergent biographies see Derek Attridge, *J. M. Coetzee and the Ethics of Reading* (Chicago and London: University of Chicago Press, 2004), 78, n.15.

7   Patrick Corcoran, "*Foe*: Metafiction and the Discourse of Power", in *Robinson Crusoe: Myths and Metamorphoses*, ed. Spaas and Stimpson, 260.

8   Charles Gildon, *The Life and Strange Surprizing Adventures of Mr. D— De F—, of London, Hosier* (London: J. Roberts, 1719), vii.

9   J. M. Coetzee, "Roads to Translation", *Tongues: Translation: Only Connect* 64.4 (2005), 145. See Kai-su Wu, "Decomposing the Authoritative Author: Truth and Confession in J. M. Coetzee's *Foe* and *Summertime*", *Tamkang Review* 43.2 (2013), 107–129.

10 J. M. Coetzee, *Foe* (1986; London: Penguin Books, 2010), 58. Subsequent citations will appear in the body of the essay. Maria Lopez reads *Foe* as a response to *Mrs Veal*: "*Foe*: A Ghost Story", *Journal of Commonwealth Literature* 45.2 (2010), 295–310.

11 Engélibert, "Daniel Defoe as Character", 271.

12 Dominic Head, *J. M. Coetzee* (1997; Cambridge: Cambridge University Press, 2010), 127. See also David Cowart, *Literary Symbiosis: The Reconfigured Text in Twentieth-Century Writing* (Athens GA and London: University of Georgia Press, 1993), 149–172.

13 Daniel Defoe, *Robinson Crusoe*, ed. Michael Shinagel, 2nd edition (New York and London: W. W. Norton, 1994), 51. On Crusoe's "autobiographical impulse" see David Marshall, "Autobiographical Acts in *Robinson Crusoe*", *ELH* 71.3 (2004), 899–920.

14 See Chris Bongie, "'Lost in the Maze of Doubting': J. M. Coetzee's *Foe* and the Politics of (Un)likeness", *Modern Fiction Studies* 39.2 (1993), 267.

15 Defoe, *Robinson Crusoe*, 51.

16 Defoe, *Robinson Crusoe*, 4.

17 Alexandra Effe, *J. M. Coetzee and the Ethics of Narrative Transgression* (Basingstoke: Palgrave Macmillan, 2017), 35.

18 Brian McHale, *Postmodernist Fiction* (1987; London and New York: Routledge, 1991), 202.

19 On Friday's enforced speechlessness see Christopher Peterson, "The Home of Friday: Coetzee's *Foe*", *Textual Practice* 30.5 (2016), 857–877, and Richard Begam, "Silence and Mut(e)ilation: White Writing in J. M. Coetzee's *Foe*", *The South Atlantic Quarterly* 93.1 (1994), 111–129.

20 J. M. Coetzee, *Stranger Shores: Essays 1986-1999* (London: Vintage, 2002), 26.

21 Annamaria Carusi, "*Foe*: The Narrative and Power", *Journal of Literary Studies* 5.2 (1989), 136.

22 Brian Macaskill and Jeanne Colleran, "Reading History, Writing Heresy: The Resistance of Representation and the Representation of Resistance in J. M. Coetzee's *Foe*", *Contemporary Literature* 33.3 (1992), 452.

23 Lewis MacLeod, "'Do We of Necessity Become Puppets in a Story?' or Narrating the World: On Speech, Silence, and Discourse in J. M. Coetzee's *Foe*", *Modern Fiction Studies* 52.1 (2006), 5.

24 Daniel Defoe, *Serious Reflections During the Life and Surprising Adventures of Robinson Crusoe* (London: W. Taylor, 1720), vii.

25 Daniel Defoe, *Roxana, The Fortunate Mistress*, ed. John Mullan (Oxford: Oxford University Press, 2008), 1.

26 Judie Newman, "Desperately Seeking Susan: J. M. Coetzee, *Robinson Crusoe* and *Roxana*", *Current Writing* 6.1 (1994), 2.

27 Defoe, *Roxana*, 6.

28 Gildon, *The Life and Strange Surprizing Adventures of Mr. D— De F—*, xvii.

29 Jane Gardam, *Crusoe's Daughter* (London: Abacus, 1985), 303.

30 See M. J. Marais, "The Deployment of Metafiction in an Aesthetics of Engagement in J. M. Coetzee's *Foe*", *Journal of Literary Studies* 5.2 (1989), 184.

31 Susan Naramore Maher, "Confronting Authority: J. M. Coetzee's *Foe* and the Remaking of *Robinson Crusoe*", *The International Fiction Review* 18.1 (1991), 39.

32 Jo Alyson Parker, "Crusoe's *Foe*, Foe's *Cruso*, and the Origins and Future of the Novel", *KronoScope* 11.1–2 (2011), 35.

33 Tisha Turk, "Intertextuality and the Collaborative Construction of Narrative: J. M. Coetzee's *Foe*", *Narrative* 19.3 (2013), 308.

34 Stuart Campbell, *Daniel Defoe's Railway Journey: A Surreal Odyssey through Modern Britain* (Dingwall: Sandstone Press, 2017), xiv. Subsequent citations appear in the body of the essay.

35 Daniel Defoe, *A Tour through the Whole Island of Great Britain*, ed. Pat Rogers (Harmondsworth: Penguin Books, 1971), 9.

3 Beyond Terracentric History

The Eighteenth-Century Slave Trade in Barry Unsworth's *Sacred Hunger*

Przemysław Uściński

The co-winner of the 1992 Booker Prize, Barry Unsworth's historical novel *Sacred Hunger* is an interesting example of neo-Georgian fiction inasmuch as it responds to questions raised by late twentieth-century critical discourses about colonialism, imperialism, race, Western culture and Eurocentrism, within an adopted conventional frame of a realist historical novel set in the mid-eighteenth century. Despite critical acclaim and the accolades it amassed, the novel has received limited scholarly attention to date. Here, I want to put under scrutiny the ways in which *Sacred Hunger* combines its tendency towards often harrowingly detailed realism with more self-reflexive intertextual techniques, so that it can critically examine the imperialist, expansionist, and racist ideologies of the Georgian period. Tellingly, the meticulous and even naturalistic account of the slave trade and the Middle Passage is tied by Unsworth's narrative with explicit or allusive references to several contemporary texts, most prominently to *The Enchanted Island* (1667), John Dryden and Sir William Davenant's adaptation of William Shakespeare's *The Tempest*, but also to the poetry of Alexander Pope and the writings of Adam Smith. Applying, among others, Michel Foucault's seminal conceptions, I focus on how the novel depicts the functioning of power and coercion, their operations through both material and discursive means, whilst, more specifically, also wanting to acknowledge that both its plot and the allusive narrative centre around the sea, thus complying with the revisionist accounts of early-modern and modern history which reject the traditional "terracentric" optics in order to appreciate the significance of the seas in shaping colonial modernity and modern globalism.[1]

The notion of "terracentric history" (a concept elaborated first by Marcus Rediker) aims to underline "the uninspected assumption that only the landed spaces on the earth's surface are real".[2] In rewriting maritime history Rediker seeks to challenge that pervasive terracentric bias "strengthened by the rise of the modern nation-state in the late eighteenth century, after which power and sovereignty would be linked to specific ethnic, civic and national definitions of 'the people' and their land, their soil". Terracentrism betrays something of the "deep structure of Western thought"; it contains "an unspoken proposition that seas are unreal spaces, voids between real spaces", while Rediker's project of reexamining "from below" what he calls "the 'age of sail', roughly 1500 to 1850" largely parallels, it seems, similar revisionist attempts within both critical postcolonial historiography and historical fiction.[3] As Homi K. Bhabha puts it in *The Location of Culture*, a national bias in history-making might be countered by the exploration of "the 'inter' – the cutting edge of translation and negotiation, the *inbetween* space – that carries the burden of the meaning of culture. It makes it possible to begin envisaging national, anti-nationalist histories of the 'people'".[4] Being real spaces, seas and oceans often render ethnic, national and linguistic boundaries fluid and problematic (Rediker speaks, for instance, of the "motley crews" on the decks of vessels crossing the Atlantic). Much like Unsworth's historical novel, as I want to argue, Rediker seeks to historicise that *concreteness* of maritime experience also because it upsets abstract categorical divisions which act as a scaffold for the discourses of territory-oriented national historiographies. For Rediker, the tangible and technological aspects of that history – including the "Northern European deep-sea sailing ship" – also speak of the decentred, *multiple* histories of the people implicated in various ways in the global narrative of "plunder, conquest, and finally a political and economic dominance that has lasted to this day".[5] As Greg Forter notes, Unsworth's novel "explores the destructiveness of racial capitalism in the eighteenth century" and depicts the effects that system has "on characters across social spectrum: middle-class professional men, enslaved Africans, European and African slave-traders, ordinary sailors, prisoners, women of various social classes, mixed-race children, and more".[6]

The plot of *Sacred Hunger* centres around a slave ship called the *Liverpool Merchant* which embarks on its maiden voyage in 1752. Commissioned by William Kemp, a soon-to-be bankrupt Liverpool merchant and father of Erasmus Kemp (Erasmus is one of the two protagonists of the novel, the other being his cousin and later nemesis, Matthew Paris, who embarks on the ship as surgeon), the vessel functions in the novel as a concrete, physical object, depicted with scrupulous attention to detail, while also becoming an emblem – an indelible and prominent metonymy – of the novel's overarching theme of the colonial slave trade. Unsworth begins his novel with a scene where adolescent Erasmus is brought by his father to witness the construction of the vessel:

> Not that there was much unusual about her. Ships had not changed significantly for a long time now. They were still built of wood, still powered by the action of the wind on sails of flax canvas attached to masts and yards supported by hemp rigging. Columbus, set down on any vessel of the time, would not have found much to puzzle him. All the same, these Liverpool ships had some special features: they were built high in the stern so that the swivel guns mounted on their quarterdecks could be the more easily, the more *commodiously* as might have been said then – a word curiously typical of the age – trained down on their waists to quell slave revolt; they had a good width of beam and a good depth to hold and they were thickened at the rails to make death leaps more difficult.
>
> Nothing very special then about the *Liverpool Merchant*. Her purpose was visible from the beginning, almost, of her construction, in the shape of her kneel, the gaunt ribs of her hull: a Liverpool snow, two-masted, brig-rigged, destined for the Atlantic trade. But Kemp's natural optimism had been inflamed to superstition by the mounting pressure of his debts, and his hope in the ship was more than commercial.[7]

While both the tangible physicality and technical efficacy of the Liverpool slave ship are underscored here, Unsworth carefully inscribes the ship within the historical contexts of geographical exploration and attendant colonialist endeavours ("Columbus [...] would not have found much to puzzle him"). Curiously, the ordinariness of the ship is referred to twice, arguably because this helps to emphasise how the technology elaborated for the purposes of the slave trade had itself already had a centuries-long tradition.[8] Since the laborious process of the construction and maintenance of the slave ship is largely a matter of routine and long-established practice, the technology of the slave ship itself naturalises the slave trade and permits William Kemp and others to sideline any potential moral quandaries: the slave ship does not obliterate slavery ("she had already the perfect dynamic of her shape, the perfect declaration of her purpose") but allows them to think of it solely in terms of logistic, technical and economic efficiency. Thurso – the pitiless, profit-driven and ruthlessly self-regarding captain of the *Liverpool Merchant* – takes evident pleasure in contemplating the ship: "Thurso listened with satisfaction to the sighing and creaking of his ship as she felt the movement of the tie beneath her. She was a good one, he knew it" (70). An already well-experienced author of historical fiction, Unsworth had researched the history of the slave trade very thoroughly, as is made evident by the descriptions of everyday life and labour on the *Liverpool Merchant* that constitute the bulk of the narrative. From the very outset of its journey, there is plenty of manual labour (tasks ranging from "plaiting rope yarns for cordage" to "stopping leaks" [11]) needed to maintain the ship which keeps the crew constantly busy and requires strict discipline.[9] As Rediker contends, "[t]he wide-ranging, well-armed slave ship was a powerful sailing *machine*", and he adds that

> it was also something more, something *sui generis* [...] It was also a factory and a prison, and in this combination lay its genius and its horror. The word "factory" came into usage in the late sixteenth century as global trade expanded. Its root word was "factor," a synonym at the time for "merchant." A factory was therefore "an establishment for traders carrying on business in a foreign country." It was a merchant's trading station.[10]

Significantly, the deck of the *Liverpool Merchant* serves in Unsworth's narrative also as a locus of chaos and rebellion – because the slave ship "needs" to be an efficient "machine", its operations require an enormous amount of brutal force, exhausting and often tedious labour, and inevitably involve much strain, sweat, danger, hunger, injury, death and corporal punishment. The slave ship as a technological development needs to be regarded as part of larger operations of power, including what Michel Foucault calls "the great carceral continuum, which provides a communication between the power of discipline and the power of the law [as] the technical and real, immediately material counterpart of that chimerical granting of the right to punish".[11] Foucault's historical analyses of the "technologies of power" focus on both the discursive and the "immediately material" aspects of their operations. Likewise, Unsworth's novel, focusing as it does on slave trade as a *legalised* and legitimised practice, is interested in what sustains power and authority as well as in what is capable of upsetting the balance of power. As Susan C. Brantly notes,

> Captain Thurso allows any form of violence to be directed towards slaves as long as it does not decrease their value. Many of his crew

have been press-ganged against their wills, and he maintains control of them through fear, punishing any signs of insubordination with a whip.[12]

Coercion depicted in Unsworth's novel aptly illustrates that *slow* transition from the cruelty of the "punishment-as-spectacle" to the more hidden, corrective and disciplining (in short: utilitarian) punitive techniques of the "carceral continuum" as discussed by Foucault.[13] There is surely much senseless cruelty (especially on Thurso's part), but violence is also strategically distributed and limited with a view to ensuring the efficiency of the slave trade – the presence of the surgeon on board to take care of the "health" of the slaves shows how cruelty was to be mitigated.

Tellingly, the mutiny that takes place at the end of Book I of the novel is *not* described – Unsworth strategically details instead all the events that lead to it, including Thurso's brutality, adverse weather conditions, navigation problems, disease, food and water shortages, and the deaths of numerous African slaves and crew members alike – events that contrast with William Kemp's optimism and the pride that Thurso takes in the ship. A catalyst for the mutiny is provided by Thurso's calculated decision to cast overboard the remaining "negroes" in order to claim insurance:

> It was a simple idea, but Thurso was a simple man, being an incarnation, really, of the profit motive [...] His idea was based on certain undeniable facts. Deaths among the negroes during the six days of bad weather had amounted to eighteen – ten men, five women and three boys. The ship had been blown considerably off course and a good number more were likely to die before Jamaica was reached. Those that survived would not look attractive to the planters that came to bid for them. Cargo dying aboard ship of so-called natural causes was quite worthless, whereas cargo cast overboard for good and sufficient reason could be classed as lawful jetsam and thirty per cent of the market value could then be claimed from the insurers.
>
> (381–382)

Thurso's "simple idea" reflects how economic profit remains the ultimate rationale for the slave trade, and the relative "simplicity" of financial calculation monstrously contrasts with the absurd enormity of violence and suffering on and below the deck of the *Liverpool Merchant*.[14] To provide one, almost random, example: McGann, one of the crew members, was "put in irons for begging rice from the bowls of negroes" – a practice stemming from the fact that crew members were often assigned even more meagre food rations than the slaves (377). As already signalled in the title of the novel, "hunger" is of momentous importance to the novel's overall artistic import: hunger is bodily, painfully experienced, and hence relates to the very material aspects of existence, but it is also "sacred" – in *Sacred Hunger* it becomes a motivation for action both in itself and as sanctioned and sanctified by ideology; it signals both deprivation and greed, and hence its "sacredness" in the novel is clearly ironic (Unsworth's irony is surreptitious, but detectable throughout the narrative).

As I want to demonstrate in my reading of the novel, its narrative dialectics rest on the negotiation between the "materially-oriented" realism of the story and the textually-oriented exposition of the contemporary rhetoric of those ideologies that underpin the very "ordinariness" of such material practices – because those tenets of the eighteenth-century slave trade are, for Unsworth, ultimately impossible to separate. The mutiny on the *Liverpool Merchant* stems from the carefully narrated despicable material conditions of the life on board and the excesses of Thurso's brutal exercise of his authority as a captain (the narrator calls those "mere savagery", adding that "there was no pretence of justice in them"). Still, however, the mutiny is actually initiated by Matthew Paris, the ship's surgeon, an educated former prisoner sensitive to human suffering and remaining under the recent influence of the revolutionary Enlightenment ideals propagated by Delblanc – the painter who embarks on the ship when it leaves the African coast, where Delblanc served as a portrait-maker for a territorial governor. It is Delblanc, in fact, who talks with some irony of the "sacred hunger":

> He was smiling slightly now but his expression was unhappy and rather bitter. "Money is sacred, as everyone knows," he said. "So then must be the hunger for it and the means we use to obtain it. Once a man is in debt he becomes a flesh and blood form of money, a walking investment. You can do what you like with him, you can work him to death or you can sell him. This cannot be called cruelty or greed because we are seeking only to recover our investment and that is a sacred duty".
>
> (325)

Here hunger stands for greed, for an excessive and "unnatural" desire ("Do you think for a moment that men would enslave one another if they lived in a state of nature?" – Delblanc later asks Paris), which the commercial, expansionist ideologies of the time make a "sacred duty". "Hunger" in the novel thus functions both as a signifier for the real material deprivation and for the monstrous greed – both for what is needed for survival and what is ferociously desired – while the two meanings are intertwined for Unsworth as they both make the hold of power and economy ever tighter. The *Liverpool Merchant* is primarily an *investment*, its ultimate purpose being the generation of profit, so that virtually everyone connected with it becomes a "walking invest-ment" – the ship's captain, the destitute sailors on board, slaves bought in order to be sold to planters, and even William Kemp as the ship's owner, who invested most of his resources in the ship – all become tied together by that "sacredness" of debt, which, once contracted, needs to be settled. An interesting example of how debt makes it possible to control and implicate the characters in colonial enterprises is provided by the figure of Governor Saunders, stationing in Africa, of whom Delblanc says:

> He will die if he does not get away from here. He would leave if he could, while he still has some chance of recovering his health, but he cannot – the Company has got him as fast *as if he were in chains*. Seventy-five pounds a year sounds well enough in Leadenhall Street. But when he got he found that it was paid in crackra [...] a kind of false currency that can only be used in the Company stores – at Company prices. It is all Saunders can do to buy cankey, palm oil and a little fish to keep himself alive. For other necessities *he has to go into debt*.
>
> (326, emphasis added)

The "sacred duty" established by debt becomes an obsession of Erasmus Kemp, William's son, after his father commits suicide upon realising that the *Liverpool Merchant* will not return and hence his bankruptcy is imminent. Erasmus Kemp blames Matthew Paris for the failure of the enterprise and, consequently, for the death of his father (even though later in the narrative it is suggested that William Kemp's debts were so substantial that even the potential profit made on the slave ship would not have saved him). Upon learning that the wreck of the ship has been located, "beached up on the south-east coast of Florida", and that stories circulate about "a kind of settlement somewhere back behind the coast, where white and black live together and no one is chief", Erasmus vows to punish his cousin and all the mutineers, and to recover at least part of the investment made by his father (427). By that time, twelve years after the mutiny onboard the *Liverpool Merchant*, Erasmus has established himself as a wealthy and influential trader, circumstances that make him even more arrogant, callous and daunting. Characteristically for his class, Erasmus thinks of his personal economic success as providing ultimate confirmation of his righteousness: "with all his opinions confirmed by increasing wealth – that infallible testimony – any slightest criticism drove him to anger" (435). Presumably, his secure financial position would make the long and dangerous expedition to St Augustine, Florida, pointless, yet for Erasmus his financial and personal losses demand revenge – recuperating the investment one way or another is not purely about rational calculation, it is a matter of justice: "Paris was necessary to the completeness of things, to the workings of justice, and so he must be there [...] Yes, the days were numbered now for cousin Matthew. *You will hang by the neck, as my father did*, he promised" (495–496).[15]

For Susan Strehle, that formidable pair in Unsworth's book – Erasmus Kemp and Matthew Paris – are constructed analogically to Marlow and Kurtz in Joseph Conrad's *Heart of Darkness* (1899), but with a twist: like Kurtz, Kemp is voracious, somewhat mysterious, and ambitious to the point of delusion; unlike him, however, "Erasmus proceeds to amass wealth in Liverpool, using civilized and legal means that comment with deadly irony on the values of European civilization".[16] Significantly for my argument, Erasmus Kemp is scarcely presented as an outspoken racist – perhaps typically of the epoch, his racism is a matter of tacit and unexamined assumptions; he thinks of the slave trade instrumentally, in terms of the larger operations of colonial capitalism, and he never actually witnesses it. In a discussion with Sir Hugo, his wealthy father-in-law, for instance, Erasmus actually advises him against acquiring more slaves:

> A negro is valuable only in terms of the work that can be got out of him in the period immediately after purchase. He is not a capital asset, the merchandise is too perishable. It is not like cattle, you cannot breed him for profit.
>
> (435–436).[17]

The obliviousness on the part of Erasmus Kemp as to what actually happens on a slave ship pointedly emphasises that such dehumanising approach to slave trade (white characters in the novel often refer to the transported slaves simply as "cargo") was conditioned partly by that wilful blindness to what the practice actually involved. Indeed, as

Rediker points out, the ignorance as to the conditions on the slave ship allowed the pro-slavery propagandists to spread misinformation:

> the official delegates from the city of Liverpool who testified in the parliamentary hearings, bravely presented the slave ship as a safe, modern, hygienic technology. Robert Norris, formerly captain and now merchant in the trade, explained to the Privy Council and the parliamentary committee that the enslaved had clean quarters (treated with frankincense and lime); good food; much music, singing, and dancing; and even luxuries: tobacco, brandy, and, for the women, beads.[18]

Sullivan, one of the crew members, is indeed employed as a musician, but he plays his fiddle when the captive Africans are daily *forced* to dance, while remaining enchained, in order to exercise their muscles.

Such blindness to the reality of the lives of people implicated in the slave trade facilitates the reductionist economic "abstraction" of human life that this trade involves – as Forter argues with reference to Thurso's and Kemp's pitiless calculations,

> [the] abstraction of human particularity into money is already a kind of death (the death of the human as sentient complexity), which murder merely actualizes [...] To capitalize one's investment in slaves is thus *at once* to reduce them to bodies and to render their bodies abstract and immaterial.[19]

Unsworth underscores the epistemic gap that allows for such double bind of "materialization" and "abstraction" by persistently interlacing, throughout the larger part of the novel, the scenes involving gruesomely naturalistic depiction of the trans-Atlantic slave trade with the decorum of the scenes of domestic life and business-making in Liverpool. Within that configuration, Erasmus's ignorance is stressed, while his point of view is also presented as thoroughly terracentric and metropolitan – he thinks in terms of land and property, wealth and territory, as when, for instance, he envisions the future prosperity of Liverpool that shall secure his own financial advancement:

> He saw a beautiful and prosperous city rising. Liverpool would be the greatest port in the land, greater than London. She would take over the Atlantic trade. All the manufacturing wealth of Lancashire would flow through her. Wolpert, he knew, had interests in coal

and in the Cheshire salt mines. Taken with the Kemp shipping and import businesses, it made a formidable combination.

(220)

Erasmus Kemp's vision of what the narrator dubs "material progress" is precisely that – the *merely material* progress as an accumulation of wealth, indeed its stark inland concentration within the confines of a metropolitan port, and much of it in his own hands. What is also note-worthy, his perspective is thoroughly patriarchal since the vision rests on his plan for combining his father's and his prospective father-in-law's businesses, thus *accumulating* wealth through primogeniture and marriage (it is not entirely clear to what extent Erasmus is interested in Wolpert's daughter, Sarah, solely on account of her father's fortune). Erasmus envisions that future *material* prosperity as simple accumula-tion, hence through the *abstraction* of materiality into property – "prop-erty" indicating *the right* to use rather than the use-value, including the right to exchange, or use through exchange, only in order to accumulate wealth ("wealth" would "flow" through Liverpool, thus enriching it). The opposition between use-value and exchange-value is discussed by Gayatri Spivak in connection with John Maxwell Coetzee's postcolonial rewriting of Daniel Defoe's *Robinson Crusoe* (1719) in his *Foe* (1986). Spivak writes:

> The undoing of the use-value/exchange-value binary repeatedly shows that for Marx, the private is defined by and contains within it the possibility of the social. The concrete individual is inherently predicated by the possibility of *abstraction*, and Marx's first great example of this is Robinson [...] In his situation, of man alone in nature, producing use-values, Robinson already of "necessity" thinks abstract labour [...] *Time*, rather than money, is the general equivalent that expresses this production.[20]

Marx emphasises that Robinson is well aware that what he is able to gather, build or produce comes from "[the] different forms of activity of one and the same Robinson, hence only different modes of human labour" – the fruits of his labour are not commodities, since their origin in human (Robinson's own) labour is not erased, but nonetheless his relations with those objects "contain all the essential determinants of value" also because he accounts for "the labour-time that specific quan-tities of these products have on average cost him".[21] Spivak suggests that Coetzee's focus on *space* rather than time allows his narrative to focus on both plurality and femininity and hence somewhat mitigate that violence of "abstraction". In contrast, in order to depict the violence of imperial capitalism, Unsworth's novel appears to purposely focus on *men* and *time*, in particular on the costly and detrimental delays in the ship's travel – and by linking time with money, it links delay with debt. Moreover, as Foucault argues, unlike the traditional ethics of the time-table, which derive from monastic practices and are based on "the principle of non-idleness", the efficiency-oriented *discipline* "arranges a positive economy; it poses a principle of a theoretically ever-growing use of time: exhaustion rather than use; it is a question of extracting, from time, ever more available moments and, from each moment, ever more useful sources".[22] This exploitative temporal logic of *exhaustion* finds its dismal illustration in both the slave trade and slavery, which, as Unsworth's novel often demonstrates, are not merely residual "practices" belonging to the pre-industrial economy; the slave trade in itself is a grand-scale, meticulously planned and ordered industry. Symptomatically, Captain Thurso is particularly enraged about delays: "to turn [the ship] from the wind meant detours and delays, and this conflicted savagely with his wish to make good time on the voyage" (113).[23]

Notably, many of the Liverpool episodes focus on young Erasmus's progress in courting of Sarah Wolpert, and his involvement to this end in the rehearsals of *The Enchanted Island*. Comprising a somewhat sentimentalised version of Shakespeare's *The Tempest* and frequently performed in the eighteenth century, the play features prominently in the narrative and "speaks to the same complex issues as the novel: the rights of Europeans to enslave Africans and to colonize land in the Caribbean and America".[24] It seems that the play also signals in the novel both the spatial and the imaginative detachment of the islanders from the gruesome realities of slavery that stand behind such questions: the trope of the "noble savage" that is suggested in *The Enchanted Island* through its slightly more affable representation of Caliban perhaps in itself indicates a delusional potential of art, even if that delusion has a utopian potential as well. Laura Brown, for instance, identifies the figure of the "noble savage" (employed by Rousseau, it can be found in the earlier "poor Indian" described by Alexander Pope in his *Essay on Man*) as symbolising a more harmonious and "natural" existence; a figure of narration to some extent alternative to the mainstream colonialist line – an alternative that valued tolerance and celebrated various manifestations of exotic otherness (it also predated the later abolitionist/anti-slavery discourses). This view, she argues, prompted the "long and complex debate about natural and revealed religion" within which some argued that the non-Christian native "others" should not be considered as excluded from salvation simply due to their "lack of access to the teachings of Christ".[25]

Nevertheless, the characters performing in the play remain largely ignorant of such potentially radical interpretations, with the notable exception of Mr Parker, the curate, who romanticises Caliban: "I am seeking to portray Caliban as debased, not in himself but by others. He is first unjustly subjected by Prospero, afterwards corrupted by the bad example of the mariners" (182). In that sense, the curate challenges what Peter Hulme and Francis Barker have identified in their important essay on Shakespeare's play as "Prospero's disavowal" of the injustice of his own act of colonial usurpation: "denial of dispossession with retrospective justification for it [...] is the characteristic trope by which European colonial regimes articulated their authority over land to which they could have no conceivable legitimate claim".[26] In Unsworth's novel, it seems, such *disavowal* of violence and usurpation functions mostly through instrumental, economically motivated justifications, so that technology, much like Prospero's magic, becomes a form of sublimation of violence, its erasure and reduction into the mere efficiency of the *machine* (Rediker's word for the slave ship), whereas *animalistic* brutality becomes ascribed to Caliban – that is, to the colonised. The curate's arguments in favour of the more humane representation of Caliban are promptly rejected by the vicar, the director of the play, who labels them as "radical ideas" and disqualifies such views by underscoring that "baptism of savages is not yet established, it is still subject to debate" (182).[27] Needless to say, Erasmus remains disinterested in the debate, as for him the rehearsals merely offer an occasion to win Sarah's affection.

If the stern Erasmus Kemp embodies in the novel the self-involvement and the wilful ignorance of the uncompromising profit-making characteristic of the class of colonial merchants, Matthew Paris stands for the more self-doubting, inquisitive and compassionate side of human nature, as promoted by some of the discourses of the Enlightenment. Following his uncle's offer, Paris enlists on the ship as a surgeon – a decision that for him is both an act of desperation and a form of self-punishment, since, after being imprisoned for refusing to withdraw his controversial scientific writings on natural evolution from publication, he lost his wife and their unborn child – a traumatic event for which Paris blames his own pride and obstinacy. As a humiliated scholar, Paris functions in the narrative both as a product of the exciting intellectual developments of the Enlightenment and a victim of a punitive, bigoted and largely anti-intellectual English society of the time. As Brantly notes, as a physician and a man of science he predictably "confronts an existential conundrum" when witnessing the inhumanity of the slave trade.[28] The books that Paris decides to take on the voyage are few: Pope, Maupertuis, Hume, Voltaire, Astley's *New Collection of Voyages and Travels*, and his own unfinished translation of Harvey's *Treatise on the Movement of the Heart & Blood*, a work "he had begun in prison" (65). There is in fact a curious, faintly ironic slippage concerning the word "heart" when Paris converses with Delblanc:

> "Yes," the painter said, with the same eagerness. "To make a good likeness you must have heart and mind working together. But the heart comes first."
>
> "The heart is a vital organ," Paris said, in his serious and slightly pedantic way. "But it is a faulty guide to conduct. It is the mind makes judgments and comparisons, furnishes evidence on which ideas of truth can be founded."
>
> "I take an opposite view," Delblanc said excitedly. "No man will ever find virtue by the mind alone – to think so was the folly of the Greeks."
>
> (328)

What Delblanc means by "heart" is "natural instinct" whereas Paris, momentarily at least, evokes the actual organ responsible for the circulation of blood he read so much about in Harvey's *Treatise*. Before that conversation, Paris is mostly dejected, reserved, and his tone usually matter-of-fact. While Paris's interests lie generally in human anatomy and natural history, Delblanc's kindness makes him revise his own "ideas of truth" and openly acknowledge that becoming the surgeon on a slave ship was a grave mistake – evoking his own experience of being pilloried and imprisoned, he says: "I knew what it is to be shackled and derided and still I came. How can that be forgiven?" (333) Consequently, Paris identifies with those "shackled and derided" and this crucial moment of identification with the victims of inhuman treatment will later translate into his solidarity with both the abused crew members and the slaves caged below the deck of the *Liverpool Merchant*. In short, both Paris and Delblanc stand in the narrative for the ambiguity and the radical potential of the Enlightenment ideals: Paris's passion for the "ideas of truth" and his occasionally "pedantic" and detached reasoning needs to be supplemented with Delblanc's utopian conceptions of kindness and equality. In that sense, Delblanc's role in the narrative is crucial, since Paris's identification with the victims of the slave trade allows him to shatter what Forter identifies as a "collective illusion" through which the abused and humiliated sailors (including Paris) are made to identify "with other white men" – and hence are prevented from perceiving the commonality between their own unbearable lot and that of the black slaves.[29] Evidently, the possibility of mutiny onboard the *Liverpool Merchant* is predicated upon the destruction of such false identification and its replacement with the solidarity based on shared vulnerability. Elsewhere, Forter observes how "the ship's very hierarchies and cruelties incubate the conditions for new, transnational solidarities and relational possibilities" since "the enslaved join the ship's (white) doctor and a radical painter aboard ship in mutinous rebellion" and subsequently "this interracial group of rebels murders the captain, runs the ship aground on the coast of Florida, and founds [there] an expressly utopian community".[30]

While racism and slavery are intertwined and mutually enforcing, Unsworth's novel depicts the slave trade also in the more broad framework of the critique of *enslavement*. When discussing the enslavement produced by contemporary society, Delbanc blames both "coercion" and the ideology of "sacred hunger" – Unsworth's novel is surely interested not only in depicting the contemporary techniques of coercion but also in examining the ideological scaffolding of the general "acceptance" for that coercion, hence addressing the question that in many ways is central to Foucault's account of the "birth of the prison" in the eighteenth century, namely: "how were people made to accept the power to punish, or quite simply, when punished, tolerate being so".[31] As I have argued so far, the novel mostly points for an answer to the brutally competitive economic system of the "sacred hunger", a phrase designating both the thirst for increasing one's wealth and the stark economic deprivation, since both tie together those collaborating in the slave trade, not least through the obligation ensuing from debt, which the novel dubs, in turn, "sacred duty". While the "sacredness" of this duty is constructed and sustained through the socially current discursive formations, including the legal system, its *enforcement* needs to be guaranteed by the coercive and frequently most brutal means: imprisoning, pillorying, hanging, flogging, beating, mutilation, shackles and chains.[32]

Although it can be argued that, as Ania Loomba writes, "[the] slave's relations with the master are markedly different than those between the worker and the capitalist", the punitive and coercive system presented by Unsworth suggests enslavement as a broader condition shared by the underprivileged.[33] As Rediker puts it, the slave ship was a "mobile, seafaring prison", and he actually mentions how "Liverpool sailors frequently noted that when they were sent to jail by tavern keepers for debt and from there bailed out by ship captains who paid their debts and took their labor, they simply exchanged one prison for another".[34]

Most of the crew are forcibly "recruited" – some of them indeed in the Liverpool taverns, through threats, violence or trickery. Deakin Britto, for instance, is "sold" to Captain Thurso by Jane, his own starving wife, for the price of two pounds. Loomba further observes that though slavery has existed outside and before global capitalism, "the slave (via the slave trade) as well as the fruits of the slave's labour enter and circulate within the global capitalist market. Mercantile capital funded the slave trade as well as the trade in plantation goods" – consequently, "[the] non-capitalist practice of slavery coexists with, feeds into, and aids, the development of capitalism".[35] Capitalism not only integrates slavery, but actually makes enslavement into a *principle* of sorts; inasmuch as labour becomes tied to capital through coercively enforceable debt, once the debt cannot be settled the debtor's labour and his or her body effectually become another's property. In a sense – to pursue that logic of the "sacredness of money" – the debt that the enslaved Africans incur follows from the substantial "investment" (the costs and the engaged resources) made by the slave traders into the venture of their transportation across the Atlantic. Erasmus Kemp, at least, seems to strongly believe this when he maniacally seeks to recoup, at least partly, his father's investment.

Poverty and debt are not, however, Paris's motivation for joining the crew of the *Liverpool Merchant*, as he himself declares: "You spoke about the need to make a living and how it inclines us to evade the truth of things, but I have not even that excuse" (329). If debt imprisons and economic necessity enslaves, this implies the hypocrisy of laissez-faire capitalism, which ostensibly promotes liberty, but leads to the exploitative rule of capital.[36] Adopting a desperate and detached "nothing-to-lose" attitude, Paris is not controlled by debt, and though initially a cynical outsider, he is gradually able to see the absurdity of the slave trade and oppose its horrifying injustice. Hence, the novel is also partly a *Bildungsroman*, inasmuch as it recounts a gradual shift in Paris's moral attitude, while his inner thoughts are brought to the readerly inspection also through the passages of his journal that interlace with the third-person narrative. The journal in fact survives in the wreck of the ship and is recovered from thence by Erasmus Kemp, who eagerly looks for the evidence of Paris's involvement in the mutiny. Erasmus manages to decipher some telling passages from the soaked leaves of its pages:

> I took Kemp's offer, not from any necessity of a material nature, but from the necessity of my shame [...] regarded myself as valueless, as disposable for any purpose, however unworthy [...] throw

my life away but I have been brought with despair to see that this was the same self-regard as before. I have assisted in the suffering inflicted on these innocent people and in so doing joined the ranks of those that degrade the unoffending [...] This has been my crime and I am more guilty in that than the common seamen, who can plead the dire necessity of [...]

(451)

Paris confesses here his guilt, which lies in forgetting that his masochistic self-effacement that prompted his joining the crew of the *Liverpool Merchant* was, paradoxically, a form of pride that combined with an utter disregard for his moral responsibilities towards others. When the survivors – both the crew and the slaves – go ashore in a remote part of Florida with the intent of living in perfect equality, Paris attempts to guard that equality and the group's isolation from the exploitative power structures that had led them onto a slave ship. When captured by Erasmus at the end of the novel, Paris realises that guilt may have been his motivation throughout:

> he had mistaken his desire to make amends for a belief in the capacities of the human spirit. And now, ragged and feverish captive, he was blundering again prating of wisdom and virtue to a man determined to believe him wicked, a man to whom virtue meant well-cut clothes, a proud bearing, money in the bank.
>
> (618–619)

Characteristically, Erasmus is outraged by what he finds in the journal, but also confused by the seemingly unreasonable, by his standards, confession made by Paris: "It struck him as verging on madness. This wild confession, this owning to a crime so outlandish, so totally different from the true ones of mutiny and theft of the negroes, outraged him with its insolence and perversity" (451). For Erasmus, his cousin Paris is guilty because he broke the law, so that the confession that admits to complicity with the law being a personal fault seems to him a form of "madness" and "perversity" – such an anti-legalist position contradicts everything Erasmus believes in: "His whole being seemed under the threat of dissolution. What became of law, of legitimacy, of established order, if a man could assume such attitudes of *private morality*, decide for himself where his fault lay?" (451, emphasis added). It is unthinkable for Erasmus that one could see law and justice as being *at odds*; as a character, he stands for the Foucauldian "carceral continuum" of power – the absolute trust in the continuity between the (moral) right to punish and the dictates of the law.[37] Such a trust excludes any possibility of "private" morality, which is seen as an imposition of arbitrary rule, a random intrusion into the order of things. Paradoxically, therefore, the seemingly anarchic brutality depicted in the novel requires for its legitimacy an unshakable confidence in order, as such confidence justifies *coercion* precisely as preventing the arbitrary (anarchic) rule of the "individual" conviction or "private" morality. The operations of that "carceral continuum" spread beyond what Foucault identifies as the eighteenth-century "great confinement" (prisons, asylums) to involve numerous institutions of discipline, correction, treatment and education. This implies that everyone is recognised by that panoply of power-knowledge structures as potentially criminal, or at least delinquent. "Delinquency" is crucial for Foucault precisely because it marks the extension of disciplinary and punitive means based on the uniformity of the "norm" *beyond* the criminal code and the punishment of crime: potential delinquency suggests recklessness (including recklessness with money – and hence *debt*) and implies the need for discipline and constant supervision.[38]

The suggestive juxtaposition of the texts of Paris's confession and Erasmus's confusion serves Unsworth to underline the difference between the two main characters, but it signals the more general thematic trajectory of the novel's plot. It brings into focus the broader reflection that the novel elaborates upon, namely the suppression of individual conscience produced through the discursive/legal framework that justifies coercive violence inasmuch as it locates the threat to order in the irregularities of individual consciousness. This suppression of conscience ultimately fails in the case of Paris – also because he cannot use economic necessity (the "sacred hunger") as his excuse, but perhaps primarily because he is able to admit to his guilt that lies there despite him actually *following* the law. Paris *refuses* to render legitimacy to his own actions merely on account that they comply with the rules of what Erasmus calls "the established order" – and this allows him to begin to dismiss the legitimacy of that order.

While Unsworth's novel surely offers an example of "postcolonial historical realism" and is "a kind of materialist anatomy of Atlantic world slavery in the eighteenth century",[39] it also provides an extensive analysis of the paradoxes of the burgeoning liberalism that masks, in fact, the extensively coercive and punitive system, which serves and "sanctifies" solely the abstracted categories of profit and property. While some characters in the novel are tempted with the promises of prosperity and advancement, most are not tempted at all, but indeed are brutally forced to partake in the atrocities of the supposedly lucrative slave trade. It is perhaps one of the overarching ironies of the novel that opposing such an overpowering and disciplining system requires the luxury of acknowledging the role of one's individual *consent*, as Matthew Paris does, and hence perhaps even one's *complicity* with that coercion which both produces and requires submissiveness.

Notes

1 I would like to express my wholehearted gratitude to Professor Jeremy Tambling for reading an early draft of this paper and sharing many insightful comments. I treasure the friendly, thought-provoking conversions we had during his frequent lecturing and teaching in Warsaw in recent years.
2 Marcus Rediker, *Outlaws of the Atlantic: Sailors, Pirates, and Motley Crews in the Age of Sail* (Boston: Beacon Press, 2014), 9.
3 Rediker, *Outlaws of the Atlantic*, 10–11. *Sacred Hunger* is often classified as an example of postcolonial historical fiction.
4 Homi K. Bhabha, *The Location of Culture* (London and New York: Routledge, 2004), 56.
5 Rediker, *Outlaws of the Atlantic*, 11.
6 Greg Forter, "Barry Unsworth and the Arts of Power: Historical Memory, Utopian Fictions", *Contemporary Literature* 51.4 (2011), 783.
7 Barry Unsworth, *Sacred Hunger* (London: Penguin Books, 1992), 9. Further references will be parenthetical.
8 According to Rediker,

> [the] origins and genesis of the slave ship as a world-changing machine go back to the late fifteenth century, when the Portuguese made their historic voyages to the west coast of Africa, where they bought gold, ivory, and human beings. These early 'explorations' marked the beginning of the Atlantic slave trade. They were made possible by a new evolution of the sailing ship, the full-rigged, three-masted carrack, the forerunner of the vessels that would eventually carry Europeans to all parts of the earth, then carry millions of Europeans and Africans to the New World.

Marcus Rediker, *The Slave Ship: A Human History* (London: Viking Penguin, 2007), 41–42.
9 Among eighteenth-century novelists it is perhaps Tobias Smollett who offers a comparable level of detail in his accounts of sea voyages, for instance in *Roderick Random* (1748), which, however, depicts slavery in a cursory manner. Tobias Smollett, *The Adventures of Roderick Random* (London, New York and Toronto: Oxford University Press, 1952).
10 Rediker, *The Slave Ship*, 44, emphasis added.
11 Michel Foucault, *Discipline and Punish. The Birth of the Prison* (New York: Vintage Books, 1995), 303. For his discussion of "machinery" in the context of disciplinary techniques, see pages 164–166.

12 Susan C. Brantly, "Engaging the Enlightenment. Tournier's *Friday*, Delblanc's *Speranza*, and Unsworth's *Sacred Hunger*", *Comparative Literature* 61.2 (2009), 136.

13 Foucault, *Discipline and Punish*, 293–308.

14 The murder scene alludes to the actual historical event – the so-called "*Zong* massacre" of 1781, later depicted in William Turner's famous painting *The Slave* Ship (*Slavers Throwing Overboard the Dead and Dying, Typhoon Coming On*) (1840). The captain of the slave ship named *Zong* decided to throw overboard sick and dying slaves (in sum 131 Africans) into the Atlantic Ocean, so that he could collect insurance money which was due only for those slaves "lost" at sea (Kenneth Morgan, *Slavery and the British Empire: From Africa to America* (Oxford and New York: Oxford University Press, 2007), 156–157). Turner's work was strongly influenced by the dramatic naval scenes depicted by the French Romantic painter Theodore Géricault, including his famous large-scale canvas, *The Raft of the Medusa* (1819).

15 According to Giorgio Agamben writing on *homo sacer*, "Not simple natural life, but life exposed to death (bare life or sacred life) is the originary political element". In Unsworth's novel the sacredness of life and the sacredness of money are ironically combined in the formula of "sacred hunger", as if suggesting (for instance through Kemp's father's suicide) how "bare life" is not actually bare, but always tied with economy and the sacredness of hunger. Still, however, Erasmus's obsession with killing Matthew Paris – his Shakespearian thirst for revenge – indicates how the economy that sanctions greed and sanctifies debt intertwines in complex ways with the (older) judicio-political patriarchal order of *patria potestas*, which Agamben identifies with "an unconditional subjection to a power of death" (Giorgio Agamben, *Homo Sacer: Sovereign Power and Bare Life* (Stanford: Stanford University Press, 1998), 44–46).

16 Susan Strehle, "Rewriting Darkness: Imperial Knowledge in Barry Unsworth's *Sacred Hunger*", *Studies in the Novel* 43.1 (2011), 79.

17 This is in response to Sir Hugo's prediction that the slave trade would soon be abolished. Indeed, the early abolitionists often had to tiptoe around the issues of the economic viability of slavery: it was often proposed at the time that the abolition of the slave trade was possible, whereas enfranchisement of the blacks was not viable (what George Boulukos calls "amelioration" tactics: the planters would need to treat the slaves they already had better and allow them to procreate). For more details on early abolitionism, see George Boulukos, *The Grateful Slave: The Emergence of Race in Eighteenth-Century British and American Culture* (Cambridge: Cambridge University Press, 2008), 201–232; Morgan, *Slavery and the British Empire*, 148-170; Brycchan Carey and Sarah Salih, "Introduction", in *Discourses of Slavery and Abolition: Britain and Its Colonies, 1760-1838*, ed. Brycchan Carey, Markman Ellis and Sarah Salih (Houndmills: Palgrave Macmillan, 2004), 1–9.

18 Rediker, *The Slave Ship*, 452.

19 Forter, "Barry Unsworth and the Arts of Power", 786.

20 Gayatri Chakravorty Spivak, "Theory in the Margin: Coetzee's *Foe* Reading Defoe's *Crusoe/Roxana*", *English in Africa* 17.2 (1990), 6–7, emphasis added.

21 Karl Marx, *Capital: A Critique of Political Economy. Volume One*, trans. Ben Fowkes (London and New York: Penguin Books, 1990), 169–170. Several pages later Marx speaks of alienation:

> Things are in themselves external to man, and therefore alienable. In order that this alienation [*Veräusserung*] may be reciprocal, it is only necessary for men to agree tacitly to treat each other as the private owners of those alienable things, and, precisely for that reason, as persons who are independent of each other

(Marx, *Capital*, 182). Slavery therefore contradicts capitalism (there is no reciprocity – slaves are not independent private owners of alienable things), while slave trade remains in line with the logic of alienation as supplemented with the logic of property, that is, the logic of an *abstract* relation which in fact regulates alienation and is able to make people into property by bestowing on slaves the legal status of alienable (sellable) "things". Needless to say, this abstraction in the case of slavery is made possible only through the use of brutal force, even though private property as such is generally admissible due to a mediating influence of a strong *moral* justification – it is seen as a protection against theft and the brutality of force.

22 Foucault, *Discipline and Punish*, 154.

23 While this logic of exhaustion applies also to space (the efficient use of the confined space on the slave ship predates the confined spaces of the prison), space gives itself less readily to such exploitative "abstraction".

24 Strehle, "Rewriting Darkness", 87.

25 Laura Brown, "Pope and the Other", in *The Cambridge Companion to Alexander Pope*, ed. Pat Rogers (Cambridge: Cambridge University Press, 2007), 223.

26 Francis Barker and Peter Hulme, "Nymphs and Reapers Heavily Vanish: The Discursive Contexts of *The Tempest*", in *Alternative Shakespeares*, ed. John Drakakis (London and New York: Routledge, 2005), 203. The importance of the image of the ship in *The Tempest* is discussed in: Elizabeth Fowler, "The Ship Adrift", in *The Tempest and Its Travels*, ed. Peter Hulme and William H. Sherman (London: Reaktion Books, 2000), 37–40.

27 As Ania Loomba reminds us: "Slavery and colonialism were often facilitated by the fiction that they were attempts to convert infidels, but in actual practice, because of the declared prohibition against Christians enslaving other Christians, slaves were often deliberately not converted, or they were converted but their papers showed their original names so that they could be bought and sold". Ania Loomba, *Colonialism/Postcolonialism* (London and New York: Routledge, 2015), 120.

28 Brantly, "Engaging the Enlightenment", 136.

29 Forter, "Barry Unsworth and the Arts of Power", 789. Although Forter associates that "collective illusion" which bounds the crew together mostly with the "brutalization" that makes the sailors, in turn, brutalise the

captured Africans (so that the sailors become complicit with the power that abuses them), his use of the phrase "white men" clearly evokes racism as an important element that strengthens this illusive identification.

30 Greg Forter, *Critique and Utopia in Postcolonial Historical Fiction: Atlantic and Other Worlds* (Oxford and New York: Oxford University Press, 2019), 29.

31 Foucault, *Discipline and Punish*, 303.

32 In one of the entries of his journal, Paris notes:

> Another man flogged today [...] This for fouling his bedding after due warning by Haines, the boatswain, who I believe is generally hated. Thomas True, the man's name. He was given a dozen lashes by our accomplished captain and unlike Wilson cried out almost from the beginning. When it was over he was not able to stand unsupported. That such cruel punishment can overcome engrained habits of uncleanliness or perhaps symptoms of some deeper disorder of mind, I do not believe. Indeed, it seems too savage a question even to speculate upon.
>
> (148)

33 Loomba, *Colonialism/Postcolonialism*, 137.

34 Rediker, *The Slave Ship*, 44.

35 Loomba, *Colonialism/Postcolonialism*, 137.

36 Adam Smith's *The Wealth of Nations* (1776) thus provides yet another important intertext for Unsworth's novel. At one point the narrator observes, alluding to Smith, that these were the times "when the individual pursuit of wealth was regarded as inherently virtuous, on the grounds that it increased the wealth and wellbeing of the community. Indeed, this process of enrichment was generally referred to as 'wealth-creation' by the theorists of the day" (158).

37 See Foucault, *Discipline and Punish*, esp. 298–308.

38 Needless to say, some groups (women, children, racial others, the poor, the mentally or sexually "deviant") become defined as requiring either confinement or correction, often by means of labour, which the bourgeois ethics elevate to the status of panacea for all possible deviations (Foucault, *Discipline and Punish*, 242–244). In the case of slavery, arguably, this disciplinary subjection turns into exploitative subjugation, though the trope of the "grateful slave" as discussed by Boulukos suggests attempted applications of that punitive utilitarian logic of "self-improvement" (part of what Foucault calls "the gentle way of punishment") also to the slaves. For a useful discussion of Foucault in the context of postcolonial theory see, for instance, Loomba, *Colonialism/Postcolonialism*, 52–60.

39 Forter, *Critique and Utopia in Postcolonial Historical Fiction*, 29.

4 "Whose Pictur'd Morals Charm the Mind / And Through the Eye Correct the Heart"[1]

Rewriting the Pictorial Narrative of *A Harlot's Progress*

M-C. Newbould

William Hogarth's *A Harlot's Progress* (painted 1731; engraved 1732), a sequence of six images depicting the archetypal story of a country ingénue coerced into prostitution upon her arrival in London, her temporary rise into wealth, then demise and death, enjoyed considerable success on its first appearance. Although the original paintings are now lost, their initial display attracted large crowds; Hogarth secured many subscribers to the promised engravings; and, when they appeared, they were so popular as to be reproduced numerous times. Celebrated acclaim can often breed creativity, and perhaps no more buoyantly than in the eighteenth century, a period during which the busy traffic between the arts thrived. *A Harlot's Progress* was adapted into new forms: images, textual narratives, musical and theatrical performances, and material objects.[2]

Although the eighteenth century was the hey-day for the images' popularity and their adaptation, *A Harlot's Progress* still continues to appeal to modern-day creators. Its narrative content, and the sometimes troubling questions it asks of its viewer, are as pertinent now as then: sexuality, exploitation, wealth, poverty, gender, and "morals". The issue of medium still lurks too: parodying the images in a painting, drawing, or caricatured print may be one thing, but how can Hogarth's visual art be transported into a non-visual medium, such as a novel, poem, or play-text? What does the adapter choose to select or to exclude, how is material re-presented, and why?[3]

David Dabydeen's *A Harlot's Progress* (1999) and Michael Dean's *I, Hogarth* (2012) evidence the enduring fascination with the *Progress* and its appeal to adaptation. Both of these novels engage with how, just as Hogarth prompted his contemporaries to re-view their immediate surroundings in startling and sometimes disturbing new ways, so his images similarly bring a modern-day audience to look at Georgian London with fresh, perhaps troubled eyes, and to hear anew the conversation between word and image in imaginative representations of lived experience.

Dabydeen tells the story of one of the seemingly marginal characters of Hogarth's sequence, the black houseboy present in the second plate (Figure 4.1) depicting Moll as a wealthy mistress. Dabydeen wrests the reader's attention from the protagonists who might first attract the viewer's gaze by giving this boy the first-person narrative voice. A former slave, Mungo is now an impoverished old man living in London; he is compelled to tell (sell) his life story to a seemingly charitable Abolitionist, Mr. Pringle. The penury and abuse he encounters are driven by racial prejudice, in a context where the wider societal, political and economic corruption of this period facilitated the exploitation of marginalised figures. For Dabydeen, the novel as an adaptation is as

Figure 4.1 William Hogarth, *A Harlot's Progress* (1732), plate 2. Etching and engraving. Harris Brisbane Dick Fund, 1932. The Metropolitan Museum of Arts.

much a response to the world that Hogarth depicts as a critique of the *Progress* itself.

Michael Dean's *I, Hogarth*, meanwhile, is a pseudo-autobiographical recreation of Hogarth's life, from early childhood struggles with poverty, to apprenticeship as an engraver, marriage, debilitating venereal disease, professional success, and an eventual fall from grace. It centres on what Dean identifies elsewhere as the "three main themes of Georgian life: money, the home, and sex".[4] He draws on the artist's own letters, contemporaneous accounts, and the abundant scholarship in the field to reconstruct how Hogarth might have been, but, more importantly, how he might have seen.[5] Hogarth's first-person voice, the titular "I", recounts his experience of his world (and the artistic images that record it) primarily gained through ocular means. Dean constructs his perception of how Hogarth saw and lived through reading a wide array of his perhaps best-known works, and converting his interpretation of what they tell into a verbal narrative.

The purpose here is two-fold. These novelistic interpretations of *A Harlot's Progress* raise questions already noted regarding adaptation in general: what, how, and why. As with other adaptations, while these two texts display fascination with their source material, both use their creative responses to Hogarth's art to foreground other preoccupations and concerns: in Dabydeen's case, racism, exploitation, marginalisation; in Dean's, how a creative genius took shape through the sensory experience of eighteenth-century London. However, the aim is also to show how, as verbal adaptations of primarily visual works, these novels provoke questions surrounding the relation between different media in representing human experience. Both Dean and Dabydeen engage with the longstanding, vexed relationship between word and image that lay at the core of eighteenth-century aesthetic theory, and of Hogarth's own work.

Rereading the Harlot's Story

It is worth recalling this wider aesthetic discourse, and Hogarth's role within it, the better to explore how these novels function as contemporary verbal adaptations of eighteenth-century visual art.[6] The extensive scholarly discussions of the disputed interaction between the so-called sister arts typically observe how throughout eighteenth-century aesthetic theory there is a recurrent emphasis on the eye as the prime organ of sight, which enables the cognitive processing of externally derived stimuli more effectively than any other sensory mechanism. Ideas, for John Locke, are inherently pictorial, "*The Pictures drawn in our Minds*";[7] any attempt to record the external world – in pictures and words – should prompt that mental image. Nevertheless (as Locke somewhat ruefully acknowledges) it cannot be assumed that words conjure the same mental picture for different individuals, nor can it be taken for granted that we all think in pictorial terms. The fascination with the eye and the recirculation of picture-oriented terminology nonetheless abound in eighteenth-century theory and practice alike. James Thomson's highly successful *The Seasons* (1726–1730) is perhaps one of the best-known literary celebrations of the eye as an agent, lifelike and potent: it is "raptur'd", "prying", "philosophic", "hurried", "ardent"; in turn, it must be "cherished", "charmed", "feasted".[8]

As Peter de Bolla argues in his richly apposite *The Education of the Eye*, Hogarth operates – and innovates – against this backdrop of popularised "metaphorics" for the eye in his *Analysis of Beauty* (1753) when he urges "the reader to assist his imagination as much as possible, in considering every object, as if his eye were placed within it".[9] Here, too, the eye is glutted by lived experience (it is "fix'd", "entertained", and "in play"), such that "Agency in the matter of vision is handed over to the ocular: the eye becomes the emperor of sight".[10] The fulcrum of de Bolla's thesis, pivoting on the eye, is his contention that

> what we have come to understand and recognise as our own modes and forms of subjectivity were first fully articulated – that is the shape and contours of the modern concept of "self" or "subject" were first intelligible as such – in the middle decades of the eighteenth century in Britain.[11]

This "articulation" took place through the gradual emergence of a complex "culture of visuality", which involved "a kind of looking" that "became a publicly available [...] form" manifested across the arts – in particular painting, architecture, and landscape gardening – that peaked mid-century.[12] Hogarth plays a significant role in this process.

Lord Kames famously gestures towards this multiplex of formative experiences in *Elements of Criticism* (1762) when he claims that "Writers of genius, sensible that the eye is the best avenue to the heart, represent every thing as passing in our sight; and, from readers or hearers, transform us as it were into spectators".[13] Dean's novel describes the switch between spectatorial roles characterising this educative immersion in the "culture of visuality" through its perceiving and describing narrator figure.[14] Dabydeen's *A Harlot's Progress*, however, challenges the terms on which the spectator and spectated upon are formed: they often inhere within power dynamics that mean some will always be excluded from this tensile reciprocity, present only as an observable and impotent object.

The interplay between passivity and the active belonging to spectatorship nevertheless performs an important function in the "pictur'd Morals" of Hogarth's art, in ways which pre-empt some of the more disturbing conclusions Dabydeen's novel addresses (and, to some degree, Dean's). Hogarth's "modern moral progresses" guide and "educate" the eye, but also demand its active employment. Hogarth achieves this by what Jenny Uglow describes as a movement "back and forth between *word* and image", which requires a particular "kind of 'reading'".[15] Indeed, as Hogarth suggests in the *Analysis*, we deploy comparable mechanisms when reading pictures and viewing texts:

> It is a pleasing labour of the mind to solve the most difficult problems; allegories and riddles, trifling as they are, afford the mind amusement: and with what delight does it follow the well-connected thread of a play, or novel, which ever increases as the plot thickens, and ends most pleas'd, when that is most distinctly unravell'd?[16]

Hogarth goes on to liken following the "thread" of a story to that of pursuing the "serpentine walk" of a landscaped garden, different art-forms colluding to create pleasing puzzles for the eye.[17] The narrative progress creates just such a stimulating environment for visual-cognitive enjoyment. The eye performs its fertile task of moving between and decoding pictorial reference points dispersed across a spatial plane, energising a form of active spectatorship that acquires a temporal quality to form a coherent visual-verbal narrative. In the first frame of *A Harlot's Progress* (Figure 4.2), in which Moll first arrives in London, we look "at" the supposedly static moment depicted, but the eye also shifts between disparate points, led (as Mark Hallett suggests) across the lines of sight established between the protagonists to create a composite mental whole.[18] The plate achieves what Ronald Paulson describes as "the movement through time in a single spatial image" to possess a form of graphic dynamism.[19]

Hallett argues that this type of reading requires proximity and participation, but also that we "stand back, both physically and metaphorically, from the individual components of the series, and come to some more abstracted conclusions about their collective meaning, context, and significance".[20] These "conclusions" include perhaps troubling self-realisations. We exercise the potent gaze and the careless glance simultaneously, engaging in a form of passive consumption inherently linked with exploitation; the spectator's eye ravages the image, just as Moll's

Figure 4.2 William Hogarth, *A Harlot's Progress* (1732), plate 1. Etching and engraving. Harris Brisbane Dick Fund, 1932. The Metropolitan Museum of Arts.

body becomes spent by the conspicuous consumerism of a buoyant sex trade.[21] The image, as much as the prostitute figure it depicts, is a consumer item fed by the market for high art on the one hand, pornographic texts and images on the other, the boundaries between the two uncomfortably conflated to involve the viewer in a disturbing complicity.[22] As David Bindman writes, "We as spectators are intended to pass from reading the prints as satires of others to seeing ourselves in the follies depicted".[23] The moral conscience of the viewer is piqued as readily as the senses are titillated, the harlot's tale yoked between condemnation and compelling attraction,[24] as the proliferation of whore narratives and images in this period suggests.[25]

This conflicted dynamic is present in both Dean's and Dabydeen's novels. They also reflect how Hogarth's "pictur'd Morals" participate in a contemporary move to challenge, entertain, and instruct using newly emerging artistic forms. Hogarth's narrative sequences of the 1730s clearly enjoy an informed conversation with the period's prose fiction,[26] following on from Defoe's landmark work of the 1720s (*Moll Flanders* particularly speaks to this context), and preceding Richardson's and Fielding's novels of the 1740s; the harlot's story is reconfigured in *Tom Jones* (1749), but also in more contentious texts such as John Cleland's *Memoirs of a Woman of Pleasure* (1748).[27] Many of these cultural products share a similar tension: they often teeter between admiring, perhaps glamorising their wicked protagonists, offering them as moral warnings, and simultaneously using them as ciphers to comment on (and critique) the wider contexts in which they operate.

It is important to recall, as Hallett stresses, that while "It is all too easy to read Hogarth as a novelist and to collapse his prints into literary formulations", he was "an artist who worked within the painted and graphic spheres of cultural production and consumption in the city", which fed off and engaged with a market predominantly invested in the visual rather than the textual.[28] There is nevertheless an interdependence between these different markets and media, both in the referential framework Hogarth deploys, and in the reception of *A Harlot's Progress*. The creative and "reading" processes alike enmesh both visual and verbal material; indeed, as Hallett prompts, Hogarth's sequence requires an "interpretive mobility" that is "amplified [...] by the dramatisation of the semiotic gaps left between the images in *A Harlot's Progress* as ones that could be replenished by a variety of representational and literary references".[29]

This impulse did not remain static within the imaginative capacities of Hogarth's contemporary viewers: *A Harlot's Progress* spawned numerous visual and verbal adaptations. Like their forbears, Dabydeen and Dean also use adaptation to profit from and to promote the popularity of Hogarth's pictorial story; at the same time, by moving a visual narrative into textual form they too invest in the interaction between different art forms that had animated the culture of visuality in Hogarth's period.

Rewriting the Harlot's Story

The second plate of *A Harlot's Progress* provides one major point of contact between Dabydeen's and Dean's novels. The viewer's attention is perhaps primarily focused on unravelling the drama of Moll, her "keeper", the departing lover, and the overturned tea-table. A monkey, entangled in the ribbons of a cap lying among the other luxury items negligently littering the scene, pulls away from the breaking crockery and the tumbling table, a moment of dynamic suspense. Moving towards this focal point is what might be taken to be another symbol of opulent excess: a small black houseboy, lavishly costumed in a turban, caught mid-air while carrying a kettle with which to refill the tea-pot.[30] All the other characters of the scene look at each other – Moll has an eye on both keeper and lover, both look at her, and the maid stares wide-eyed at the young man – but the servant boy looks only at the overturning tea-table, and perhaps beyond it at the monkey, which turns to look behind itself. The houseboy is implicitly associated with objects of servitude (the tea paraphernalia), of wealth (the tea itself; the ornate furniture), and of exoticism in the monkey, a notoriously capricious creature.

The image is well-known;[31] however, its very familiarity provides Dabydeen with a starting-point for interrogating the stories lost within Moll's more prominent narrative. Yet in amplifying what might be a sub-text, Dabydeen also draws attention to the problematic reasons why the houseboy's story might only be considered peripheral. The comparative dearth of black faces in eighteenth-century art (especially when depicted in roles other than those of servitude), or in the imaginative literature of the period, exposes not only its racial inequity but also that perpetuated by observers of and commentators on these cultural products, then and now. As Dabydeen argues in his academic work on the subject, Hogarth "was the most prolific painter and engraver of blacks" of his day; it is the "*colour-blindness*" of scholarship which ignores this.[32] As such, the author is arguably less interested in Hogarth's work itself than in what an adaptation of it might highlight. Indeed, according to Abigail Ward, Dabydeen is "less directly preoccupied with art and artists" here than in his other works, though he remains "both fascinated and worried by the production and continued reception of representations of black people".[33] In basing his novel on this "minor" black character of Hogarth's *Harlot's Progress*, Dabydeen draws attention to a typically neglected story within the overarching narrative of eighteenth-century life.

This apparently voiceless character, whose mouth is open but whom the context seems to deny any articulate sound, becomes the narrator and chief protagonist of Dabydeen's *Harlot's Progress*. Mungo's story intertwines memories of his childhood home in Africa before his abduction and coercion into slavery, first on board a slave ship, then in England. Sold into the service of a high society family, the abuse and exploitation he has experienced up to this point continues in new forms; he is "saved" from a London auction but his deliverance is questionable:[34] "Lord Montague himself buy me and I praise God for the room pack with men with red faces and wild looks as if they come to eat me, a fattened calf or suckling pig".[35] He becomes another fashionable acquirement, again aligned with "*things*, a relation that is indicative of the depersonalisation of human life",[36] as Dabydeen writes. He is physically and sexually abused, considered amusing but of less intrinsic worth than Lady Montague's now-dead pet monkey: "At least the monkey moaned and even fainted when she taunted him" (213), Lizzie the servant notes with disappointment. In each stage of his story, Mungo experiences only new iterations of what slavery encompasses.

The under-representation of black lives in art and its scholarship, and the widespread racial abuse individuals such as Mungo experienced in this period, are key to Dabydeen's repurposing of Hogarth. However, although this novel has often been discussed primarily from postcolonial perspectives, *A Harlot's Progress* might also be approached following the author's suggestion that "an even deeper corruption in English (and European) treatment of blacks [...] is the corruption of commercialism".[37] While evident in the different versions of enslavement Mungo experiences, this wider economic and social discourse also negatively determines the lives of the many marginalised individuals with whom he builds a network of sympathetic, if conditional, connections, in particular Moll herself. Sexual abuse and exploitation characterise both their experiences.[38] Dabydeen argues that Moll is also subject to one form of "slavery", the victim "descended upon by vultures who will exploit her sexually and economically", as much a kept creature as her pet monkey: she is disenfranchised by the economic hardship suffered under Robert Walpole's government (the true target of Hogarth's satire in *A Harlot's Progress*).[39] His novel verbally enacts how Hogarth's art champions "the lives of the common people in a serious and sympathetic way", and so "invests their lives with significance".[40] It brings into view all those for whom thriving eighteenth-century Britain was a corrupt, disease-ridden, and unforgiving place.

While distinct racial and gendered experiences must not be crudely merged, Dabydeen nevertheless juxtaposes them the better to compare the exploitation Moll and Mungo separately experience within this wider social context, such that the ambiguity of his novel's title (applicable to both characters alike) acquires a particular poignancy. Its final section brings these trajectories into closer parallel as the narrator nurses the disease-ridden, dying Moll: she rapidly declines, her wrapped-up body verbally pictured as it appears in the fifth plate of Hogarth's sequence. She has been "saved" by Gideon, the Jewish merchant depicted in the second scene, which is perhaps Dabydeen's way of recuperating another minority "type" subjected to the artist's satire from contemporary racial discrimination: Hogarth was "shamelessly and greedily capitalizing on popular prejudice against the Jew by depicting him in a contemptuous light".[41] If, as Dabydeen suggests (following Ronald Paulson), Hogarth's Jew is based on Walpole's ally Sampson Gideon, crude stereotyping lends edge to the political critique.[42]

The spiritual ascendancy of Moll's final demise is attended by Mungo's devout ministrations, to reach a separation between body and soul which, perhaps, some might have considered impossible for the "fallen" prostitute. This Moll is Clarissa-like: more sinned against than sinning. Dabydeen's narrator looks beneath her shroud and describes not the festering flesh of the corrupted woman, but wholeness:

> I had expected to lift the blanket to a sight piteous beyond words, but was faced instead by unblemished form. Her disease, though it raged violently within her, could not break through to the surface of her. She was the very image of the Virgin depicted in many of Lord Montague's paintings.

(270)

However, the ambiguous altruism of sympathy (and of spirituality) surfaces in Mungo's devotion to Moll, in its unsettling proximity between religious and sexual ecstasy: "In her final days I took advantage of her weakness by throwing off her blanket and lifting her bodily to the tub to be bathed" (270). Mungo's self-identification with Christ up to this point becomes compromised by his own participation in Moll's abuse; his "hands" having fervently "explored all the nakedness of her", he transfers divine transcendence onto her: "It was the helpless beautiful body of a harlot which, after I had done with it, I lifted out of the tub with remorse as final as that of the apostle as he lifted Christ's corpse from Calvary" (270). Spectatorial roles become merged, he gazing on her, she on him; but this is not a moment of reciprocal, sympathetic exchange; nor is it one of empowerment on either side. Instead, it attains an ambiguous deferral of spectatorial power to an unknown, transcendent, but absent other. This Moll is a Madonna-like icon (just as Hogarth's Moll is modelled on high-art depictions of her uncorrupted namesake, Mary[43]); she is closely connected with the supplicant as their intermediary, though detached and remote – but she is also effectively powerless.

Dean is similarly drawn by the ambiguous "moral" of *A Harlot's Progress*, and how Moll's sexualisation is the product of the wider corrupt economies in which she necessarily participates. He disperses features of the sequence across his novel. Just as Moll Hackabout fascinates Dabydeen's narrator, so here the harlot is a recurrent reference point in the unfurling scenes of the artist's life. He first meets her as a boy when he accompanies his mother to seek a loan from Moses/Alexander da Costa, the Jewish merchant depicted in Hogarth's second plate. Dean singles out and carefully describes details that attract the nascent artist's eye to be stored, revisited, and reused at a later date, thereby encouraging the reader to picture the scene for themselves. The black houseboy is parcelled in with "such beauty, such luxury, such taste", as the mature artist ironically recalls the easily charmed wonder of his adolescent self. He notices the boy as just one among several unusual objects in da Costa's drawing room:

> Oh, there was so much new experience for me in this one chamber of marvels; I had heard of blackamoors – who hasn't? But there, in a corner, was an exquisite miniature man, black as ebony and carrying a copper kettle, ready to replenish, as I supposed, his master's drink. And tied to the table there was a monkey. I wager it was the only monkey in Spitalfields, perhaps in all of London, certainly the only one I had ever seen.
>
> (27)

Again, there is the equation between human being, material object, and non-human animal; the monkey is apparently even more remarkable and unique than the "blackamoor", who is demeaningly toy-like, an "exquisite miniature man", his "ebony" skin a cheapening label for all the value of the material itself. The eye of Dean's narrator is more intrigued by the paler flesh of the sensual hostess Kate, as Moll is named in the novel.[44] She is saucy and coquettish, surprising the adolescent Hogarth with an erection. The fleshliness of her body, indeed, causes him almost not to be able to see, exciting a visual and sensory experience in which the busy, consuming eye temporarily becomes inanimate:

> But the most marvellous wonder, for the *tabula rasa* of a boy that I then was, was sitting across from the Jew, to his right. She had a round, sweet face beneath her bonnet, a black patch just right of centre on her forehead, a bow of a mouth, an old gold dress of Spitalfields silk faced with white lace, pretty little red shoes.
>   But none of that was what stopped my heart; drained my mouth of spit, like I'd just eaten a sour Maidstone apple; widened my eyes to pebbles. The skin of her arms and neck was white but with the depth of cream.
>
> (27–28)

The fairly conventional blazon first situates Kate alongside the other objects in the room, its "ebony" servant included, as the narrator enumerates her outward features, noticing contrasts of colour – black, white, red – that reduce the woman to a painterly schema. The turn between the two "But[s]" of this passage, however, infuses the portrait with animate life even as it seems to seep vitality from the artist who paints it: his heart pauses; his mouth dries; his eyes widen to become "pebbles"; but the bland, non-descriptive "white" richens into "cream". Hogarth's "*tabula rasa*" rapidly fills with "new experience" that goes beyond the visual accumulation of details as his eye touches upon and penetratively participates in the object of his regard. As Claude Gandelman claims, "The eye is a tactile creature, an agent of human contact. By virtue of its mere touch, the eye gives life".[45]

Although Kate remains a lingering presence in Hogarth's "imagination" she eventually fades from view, like Moll herself. She is nevertheless vital in shaping the artist's perceptive capacities in a way that informs his future work. The impression she creates compiles with a myriad of sensory experiences that Hogarth accumulates as he makes his way through the compelling, consuming environment of eighteenth-century London. He acts as a reporter who observes, records, and shows with speedy execution: "When I drew I wanted to catch the passing moment, quick, quick, quick, not scratch away laboriously like a whore with the clap, easing her itch" (73), such as characterises the frustratingly painstaking task of the engraver. His imagination becomes practised such that "I no longer drew from life at all, instead training myself to memorise a scene, then sketch the story of it later" (57). As Addison suggests, "the Fancy" makes "Scenes [...] which were at first pleasant to behold, appear more so upon reflection", as "the memory heightens the delightfulness of the original".[46] The novel's successful ekphrasis, however, relies on language to conjure this "delightfulness" to the mind's eye; as Addison also claims, "Words, when well chosen, have so great a force in them that a description often gives us more lively ideas than the sight of things themselves".[47]

In this respect, Dean's novel differs markedly from Dabydeen's in terms of its focus and style: each adaptation sees different things in (or absent from) Hogarth's *A Harlot's Progress* and repurposes it to create alternative narrative possibilities for where it might go next in its variant afterlives. This rests on how each author "reads" Hogarth as a visual text that can be "translated" into words, or as a hybrid of different modes of reading, interpretation, and re-presentation – the "back and forth" between word and image that Uglow describes. This is not a linear process, but a dynamic, reciprocal interchange between different media and ways of seeing. As with many adaptations, *I, Hogarth* can make sense without direct knowledge of its source(s), as in, Hogarth's works; but if the reader-viewer completes the loop to picture the artist's picturing of such scenes, the reading experience brings the pleasure of recognising both similarity and change.

Dabydeen's *A Harlot's Progress* is perhaps more heavily invested in language as language, rather than as ekphrastic vehicle; it does engage with words' ability to serve as pictorial tools that conjure mental images, but the real interest comes in how language serves a personal and a social function. It is the means for self-expression, but also for a cultural self-identification that is frequently allied to a sense of place – of home, country, perhaps continent – with the interfamilial, professional, and friendship bonds that require and determine language use. Mungo is uprooted from those environments in which linguistic identity is generated and secured. In telling his life story to Mr. Pringle he must negotiate a vexed mechanism for self-expression that is intimately bound up with the terms of enslavement that have negatively conditioned that personal experience. He must communicate it in the alien tongue of his oppressors, affirming Mungo's ruptured African identity. The value of language as a liberating tool for self-expression and communication is questionable when the terms on which words are exacted, spent, and recirculated are complicit within a wider system of problematic "morality".

Mungo anticipates that his pseudo-editor will sanitise some aspects of his story while enhancing others to prompt his readers' conscience into supporting a good cause, as the novel's neologistic opening sentence indicates: "Put this down in your book Mr Pringle, properize it in your best English" (11). The reader is subsequently switched between different voices, sometimes mid-sentence, a striking feature of *A Harlot's Progress* which seems particularly to have attracted its reviewers' attention.[48] The effect can be disorienting. On the one hand, it confirms Mungo's consignment to a cycle of different versions of slavery. He tells his story for a charity that will thrive on making a prurient spectacle of the "typical" abused slave; it is as though, Tom Keymer writes, "the identity that Mungo's patron seeks to foist on him would amount to further enslavement".[49] He is "Mungo", or "Noah", or "Perseus", as various Crusoe-figures attempt to control his narrative:

A black boy, fish-meal at best, one–two small English words in my mouth which Betty learn me, just enough to tell me who I am – nit, pit, slug, dung – one–two small English words like coppers that weigh down the eyelids of the dead.

(185)

On the other hand, Mungo's mastery of English but also of multiple tongues gives him a form of empowerment over his immediate and possible future audiences. He consciously mimics the supposed voice of the African slave for Mr. Pringle's benefit to satisfy pre-existing expectations, but also deliberately to waylay those preconceptions. Mungo's linguistic manipulation allows him a supple control over the story he is willing to tell. He tends to withhold rather than provide information, despite his interviewer's hungry if restrained impatience, repeatedly invoking inexpressibility – "do not ask me..." – not to indicate incapacity, but potency. Mungo's repeated command taunts his patron: "Properize this in your English, Mr Pringle, put in your book the noise of the scream, the knives how they wade in and out of flesh like happy bathers", before rendering an eloquent memory of his childhood home (22).

Mungo exposes how the "English" view of his enslavement aestheticises it as both repellent and horribly fascinating. He ironically undercuts the aesthetic appeal of himself and his story, subverting the conventions of abolitionist texts which deploy scenes of suffering to incite sympathetic compassion while also (perhaps) stirring interest in it; Hannah More's *Slavery: A Poem* (1788) graphically pictures the tortured slave: "the sharp iron wounds his inmost soul, / And his strain'd eyes in burning anguish roll".[50] But, as we have seen, the act of spectatorship is far from straightforward. As More admits, "Whene'er to Afric's shores I turn my eyes, / Horrors of deepest, deadliest guilt arise".[51] Not the thing itself but an imagined version of it conjures a self-reflexive ethical response. Does intensifying scenes of horror serve the compassionate ends of sensibility, assuage "guilt", or draw the detached spectator into a troublingly pleasurable engagement with them? Perhaps a combination of all these things.

A Harlot's Progress is thus highly conscious of the existing matrix of expression (and expectation) in which this story operates, but also the conditional authenticity it thereby acquires. As Ward argues, it follows the arc traced by many eighteenth-century slave narratives, which effectively meant that "slaves were, like books, read and consumed by an audience [...] they were part of a process of representing black people which was not devoid of exploitation".[52] Various by-products of corruption within this context are interlinked, as Dabydeen suggests: slaves, prostitutes, the things money can buy, including books, pictures, and charitable sympathy. When Mungo denies Mr. Pringle some of the more thrilling details he evidently craves, he suggests once again the hypocrisy of charitable benevolence, rendered cheap within an economy where the luxury of sympathy is most available to those who can afford to indulge in it:

Mr Pringle puts his hand in his pocket, as if to hide his disappointment. I notice his hand bunch uncharitably around the coin in his pocket, the coin he has reserved for me but which he will not now surrender, for I have left him dissatisfied.

(178)

Readers familiar with Hogarth's *Harlot's Progress* may well associate this gesture with those of the various male hands which suspiciously travel into their own pockets, or under women's skirts, the "purses" found within them notoriously aligning money, sex, people, things. In fact, the protagonists of eighteenth-century England are all subject to the particularised economies in which they necessarily operate – of vast wealth, of poverty, of charitable organisations, of the sex, book, and slave trades – all of which are interconnected, and which render the "human" component serviceable only to the ends of dubious interests. These contexts should not excuse the need to exercise moral responsibility, but they often do. "Thing" acquires a value-less relation with "word"; words' ability to convey truth, meaning, or authentic substance becomes as false as the object, book, or art-work that circulates on a commodity market where "value" holds no true currency.

Are language, value(s), and human communication (in person, print, or paint) more stable in Dean's novel? He acknowledges the necessarily commercialised markets for paintings, engravings, and books, and that they are inevitably flawed instruments for conveying human experience. There is, of course, slippage between things and the words or images used to represent them, and some tacit acknowledgement of the power structures inherent in linguistic (and commercial) systems of expression. But for Dean's narrator unstable language is not a source of Lockean, anxious inexpressibility. Ambiguity nurtures imaginative play between image, word, idea, and meaning. "Afternoon, Sadler's Wells" (one of the *Four Times of the Day* (1736)) illustrates the point. Hogarth, presiding over his artist friends at Old Slaughter's, sketches a man bearing horns on his head – prompting the conventional connection with cuckoldry – only then to confuse the reading by adding the body of a cow behind him and his wife.

"So, is he still a cuckold?" asked Thomas Hudson.

"Aye, there's the rub," said I. "Because I no longer know. And neither do you. The man might be a cuckold. Or he might just be standing in front of a cow. So our *deception* has created *uncertainty*. And why is uncertainty good art, gentlemen? [...] Because it is interesting. The repetition of an old truth is not interesting. It is stale. The creation of a new truth is more interesting. But the most interesting is the creation of a new uncertainty".

(163–164)

Ambiguity creates fruitful possibilities rather than undermining truth. The "moral" may be harder to decipher, or indeed multiple, but it is present nonetheless.

The same, of course, could be said of Dabydeen's text: its moral purpose is clear, even if it exposes its own expressive tools as untrustworthy. For Dean's protagonist, however, the lens through which he views and conveys experience and moral purpose alike is inevitably profoundly distinct from that of Dabydeen's narrator. The white male of eighteenth-century London is bound to see and benefit from the value of words and images in a fundamentally different way to the former slave. This breeds a certain confidence of character, but also of faith in the methods for self-expression, which Dean robustly conveys. There is no slippage between ambiguous narrative registers here, for "Hogarth's" voice is decidedly his own as Dean explores an emergent subjectivity shaped by participating in a culture of visuality that requires a consciousness of seeing, being seen, and being a creator of the seen. But this Hogarth, in his lusty engagement with the pleasures, temptations, and vicissitudes of London, also embodies the hypocritical duality of the spectator-participant that views his progresses: carelessly whoring the one moment, compassionately supporting the Foundling Hospital the next, or viewing Moll Hackabout with sympathetic ambivalence.[53]

That the bluff self-confidence of Dean's Hogarth and the thoughtful doubt of Dabydeen's Mungo may lie at odds returns to the essential inequalities conditioning life for the actual participants behind these stories. Hogarth's very real experience of poverty drives the sympathy Dabydeen identifies in his depictions of "the common people". Is he nevertheless always at a privileged remove by virtue of his gender, his race, and his eventual financial success? Sex may be dangerous for Hogarth – the tragedy of childlessness which sours his marriage is caused by venereal disease – but it is also abundantly pleasurable (as Dean's novel relishes), and not a necessity, as it is for the numerous prostitutes he employs, or even for the servant girls who rely on his patronage. It is not an even playing-field. Yet as the declining Hogarth of Dean's novel shows, now out of favour with the public thanks to changing times and a hostile campaign led by John Wilkes, few remain safe from the inequalities of an imbalanced social system. The commercial rapacity of the eighteenth-century culture of visuality sells consumerism as empowerment, but effectively enslaves the producer and consumer, the spectator and spectated upon alike.

Acknowledgement

"Research for this chapter was funded by the National Science Centre, Poland, as part of the Opus project number 2020/37/B/HS2/02093."

Notes

1 From David Garrick's epigraph on Hogarth's tombstone.
2 The main scholarly sources used here that discuss *A Harlot Progress*, addressed in further detail below, are David Bindman, *Hogarth* (London: Thames and Hudson, 1981); Ronald Paulson, *Hogarth: The "Modern Moral Subject" 1607-1732* (New Brunswick and London: Rutgers University Press, 1991); Mark Hallett, *The Spectacle of Difference: Graphic Satire in the Age of Hogarth* (New Haven: Yale University Press, 1999).
3 See, for instance, Linda Hutcheon, *A Theory of Adaptation* (London: Routledge, 2006), xi–xvi.
4 Michael Dean, *I, Hogarth* (New York and London: Overlook Duckworth, 2012), 261. Subsequent page numbers are given in parentheses in the text. Michael Dean, "William Hogarth and Georgian Life", *History Today*, 24 September 2012. www.historytoday.com/blog/2012/09/william-hogarth-and-georgian-life accessed 06/11/2019.
5 An afterword indicates Dean's scholarly sources.
6 Relevant work includes Jean H. Hagstrum, *The Sister Arts: The Tradition of Literary Pictorialism and English Poetry from Dryden to Gray* (Chicago: University of Chicago Press, 1958); Richard Wendorf (ed.), *Articulate Images: The Sister Arts from Hogarth to Tennyson* (Minneapolis: University of Minnesota Press, 1983); David Marshall and Dean Mace, "Literature and the Other Arts", in *The Cambridge History of Literary Criticism: The Eighteenth Century*, vol. 4, ed. H. B. Nisbet and Claude Rawson (Cambridge: Cambridge University Press, 1997; online, 2008), 681–740.
7 John Locke, *An Essay concerning Human Understanding*, ed. Peter H. Nidditch (Oxford: Oxford University Press, 1975), 152.
8 James Thomson, "Spring", *The Seasons*, ed. James Sambrook (Oxford: Clarendon, 1981). These terms are interspersed across the poem.
9 William Hogarth, *The Analysis of Beauty*, ed. Ronald Paulson (New Haven and London: Yale University Press, 1997), 22; cf. xxxvii. See also Peter de Bolla, *The Education of the Eye: Painting, Landscape, and Architecture in Eighteenth-Century Britain* (Stanford: Stanford University Press, 2003), 25–28.
10 De Bolla, *Education*, 26.
11 De Bolla, *Education*, 4.
12 De Bolla, *Education*, 4–5.

13 Lord Kames, *Elements of Criticism*, cited in David Marshall, *The Frame of Art: Fictions of Aesthetic Experience, 1750–1815* (Baltimore: The Johns Hopkins University Press, 2005), 43.

14 Jenny Uglow discusses how Hogarth grew up and lived in "a visual age" in *Hogarth: A Life and a World* (London: Faber, 1997), xv.

15 Uglow, *Hogarth*, xv. On "reading" the *Progress*, see Bindman, *Hogarth*, 55.

16 Hogarth, *Analysis*, 33.

17 See Paulson, *Hogarth*, 260–269.

18 Hallett, *Spectacle*, 123–124.

19 Paulson, *Hogarth*, 265.

20 Hallett, *Spectacle*, 125.

21 Hallett, *Spectacle*, 99–105, 112. See also Jakub Lipski, *Painting the Novel: Pictorial Discourse in Eighteenth-Century English Fiction* (London and New York: Routledge, 2018), 64.

22 Hallett, *Spectacle*, 124.

23 Bindman, *Hogarth*, 89.

24 Paulson (ed.), Hogarth, *Analysis*, xxx–xxxi. Hallett, *Spectacle*, 112.

25 Paulson, *Hogarth*, 238–240, 256–300.

26 Hallett, *Spectacle*, 119–123. Uglow likens Hogarth's immediacy to Richardson's "writing for the moment" [sic], especially in *Pamela*; *Hogarth*, 56.

27 Peter Jan de Voogd, *Henry Fielding and William Hogarth: The Correspondences of the Arts* (Amsterdam: Rodopi, 1981), 57–58. Bindman, *Hogarth*, 55. The progresses have also been likened to proto-graphic novels, comic strips, and filmic sequences. See Lipski, *Painting the Novel*, 63–65; Stephen Moore, *The Novel: An Alternative History, 1600-1800*, 701–702; Thierry Smolderen, *The Origins of Comics: From William Hogarth to Winsor McCay* (Jackson: University Press of Mississippi, 2014), 3ff. Andrea Wulf likens them to "the scenes of a play", a theatrical metaphor Hogarth himself favoured; "A Rake's Progress", *New York Times*, 1 February 2013. www.nytimes.com/2013/02/03/books/review/i-hogarth-by-michael-dean.html.

28 Hallett, *Spectacle*, 106.

29 Hallett, *Spectacle*, 125.

30 As Dabydeen writes, a "black houseboy" was a fashionable acquisition; *Hogarth's Blacks: Images of Blacks in Eighteenth-Century English Art* (Manchester: Manchester University Press, 1987), 17.

31 Bindman, *Hogarth*, 56–57; Paulson, *Hogarth*, 265–268; Hallett, *Spectacle*, 96.

32 David Dabydeen, *Hogarth's Blacks: Images of Blacks in Eighteenth-Century English Art* (Manchester: Manchester University Press, 1987), 9.

33 Abigail Ward, "David Dabydeen's *A Harlot's Progress*", *Journal of Postcolonial Writing* 43.1 (2007), 32.

34 Ward, "David Dabydeen's *A Harlot's Progress*", 38.

35 David Dabydeen, *A Harlot's Progress* (London: Vintage, 2000; first pub. 1999), 173. Subsequent page numbers are given in parentheses in the text.

36 Dabydeen, *Hogarth's Blacks*, 11.

37 Dabydeen, *Hogarth's Blacks*, 36.

38 Dabydeen, *Hogarth's Blacks*, 36.

39 David Dabydeen, *Hogarth, Walpole and Commercial Britain* (London: Hansib, 1987), 87, 107–108, 11. See also Paulson, *Hogarth*, 248–250.

40 Dabydeen, *Hogarth's Blacks*, 11.

41 Dabydeen, *Hogarth, Walpole*, 109.

42 Dabydeen, *Hogarth, Walpole*, 111–112.

43 Hallett, *Spectacle*, 115–116.

44 A real-life prostitute, Katherine (Kate) Hackabout, was apprehended and sentenced to hard labour in Bridewell by John Gonson. See Ronald Paulson, *Hogarth: His Life, Art, and Times*, abridged by Anne Wilde (New Haven and London: Yale University Press, 1974), 107–108.

45 Claude Gandelman, *Reading Pictures, Viewing Texts* (Bloomington and Indiana: Indiana University Press, 1991), 1.

46 Joseph Addison, *Spectator*, 417, Saturday 28 June (1712), in *Critical Essays from the Spectator by Joseph Addison: with four Essays by Richard Steele*, ed. D. F. Bond (Oxford University Press, 1970), 194.

47 Addison, *Spectator*, 416, Friday June 27 (1712), in *Critical Essays*, ed. D. F. Bond, 192.

48 For instance, see James Hopkin, "Mungo the Master", *The Guardian*, 22 May 1999, www.theguardian.com/books/1999/may/22/books.guardianreview21; Hilary Mantel, "Guilt around the pictureframe", *The Independent*, 22 May 1999, www.independent.co.uk/arts-entertainment/books-guilt-around-the-picture-frame-a-harlots-progress-by-david-dabydeen-jonathan-cape-pounds-10-1095106.html; *Goodreads*, www.goodreads.com/book/show/875826.A_Harlot_s_Progress.

49 Tom Keymer, "Slave and whore", *The Times Literary Supplement*, 7 May 1999, 22. *The Times Literary Supplement Historical Archive*, http://tinyurl.gale.com.ezp.lib.cam.ac.uk/tinyurl/C9Xkc7.

50 Hannah More, *Slavery: A Poem* (London, 1788), 13. See also Markman Ellis, *The Politics of Slavery: Race, Gender and Commerce in the Sentimental Novel* (Cambridge: Cambridge University Press, 1996), 6.

51 More, *Slavery*, 7.

52 Ward, "David Dabydeen's *A Harlot's Progress*", 33–35, 37.

53 On this duality, see Wulf, "A Rake's Progress".

5 The Blind Man and the Rainbow

Vicarious Experience and Libertinism in *The Skull and the Nightingale*

Tymon Adamczewski

The premise of Michael Irwin's 2013 novel is fairly simple – after returning to London from the Grand Tour, Richard Fenwick, a dashing 23-year-old rake, is sponsored by his uncle to lead a double life in the capital and to report on his amorous conquests. Not surprisingly, these exploits are connected with a hedonistic lifestyle and a gradually progressing involvement in dubious moral affairs. Offering a swiftly written rendition of 1760s England, *The Skull and the Nightingale* successfully imitates classical literary works of the period and their literary culture to probe the complexities of vicarious experience, both for the wealthy but sociopathic uncle and for the readers, who are promised a look into human passions. Through its convoluted structural layering and elaborate plotting, the novel not only investigates the possibilities of narrating experience though letters but also depicts power-laden social relationships which serve as a metaphor for the links between the writer, the reader and the written word. Yet while such literary records of pleasure-seeking might have played the very specific role of teasing out moral and political boundaries of the eighteenth-century public (e.g. libertine fiction), the present-day imitations of such writing invite critical considerations, not least about their effect and purpose.

While for some more outwardly political positions, such as feminist discourses, rewriting the past through erstwhile literary forms was an explicitly political act, a seemingly straightforward imitation nowadays seems more problematic. Presently, any such attempts need to be situated also within the broader trend of contemporary culture's nostalgic obsessions, often expressed in the growing popularity of various retro trends: from vintage design (architecture, clothes, furniture, etc.) through vinyl records to media stylistics. This tendency includes period- or decade-driven textual production which, in one way or another, offers to (re)construct the past and is frequently informed by a relation to aspects of representation, identity or gender. One of the most pronounced examples of this tendency is visible in neo-Victorian works, with several celebrated authors situating their contemporary reworkings of nineteenth-century fiction in relation to their own academic background. A.S. Byatt, Sarah Waters or Margaret Atwood, for example, often include mis- or underrepresented minorities in their writing and orient their prose more or less explicitly in relation to academic theorising.[1]

At first glance, *The Skull and the Nightingale* seems to fit into a similar string of explorations in scholarship-fiction relations but, in this case, set in the eighteenth century. It is one of the more popular books written by Michael Irwin (b. 1934) – British Emeritus Professor of English at the University of Kent, who also worked at various institutions of higher education around the world (Poland, Japan and the US) – and aptly reflects his academic interests in Enlightenment culture. Moreover, it corresponds to his published research on the significant personages of the era (Defoe, Pope, Richardson, Fielding, Sterne, Smollett and Johnson), but as an example of a text directed to a broader audience, the novel fits into the various versions of contemporary historical fiction (e.g. J. M. Coetzee's *Foe*, Catherine Czerkawska's *The Jewel*, Francis Spufford's *Golden Hill*, to name but a few). Like other works of this genre, Irwin's novel – with its impressive imitation of the late eighteenth-century world, knowledgeable reliance on the epistolary stylistics and skilfully employed period poetics – offers a chance to revisit the era. However, it equally expresses a veiled but sustained interest not so much in terms of any (identity) politics but more in contemporary aspects of fiction, especially those concerning reader-narrative positioning and the exploration of aspects of textual immersion.

Despite its historicised setting, Irwin's work does not seem to put forward any concrete agenda for its retro poetics (political, didactic or otherwise) but intentionally basks in its simulated period potential. This is done in a way which differs from more engaged travesties of the past, visible for instance in much of postmodern fiction. Although one can find postmodern tactics in the novel (e.g. versions of metafiction or self-referentiality), they remain ostentatiously rooted in old-fashioned poetics and seem intent more on anachronistic retrospection rather than pastiche. The contemporary positioning of intertextuality and the modern conceptualisation of Enlightenment rationality contribute to breaking up of historical time, which results in what Fredric Jameson identified some time ago as the nostalgia mode – stylistic reliance on re-enacting the past through constructing a simulated image of a given historical period.[2] However, while such historicising might easily suggest a nostalgic longing for the past (fascination with the eighteenth century) and thus indicate a mere psychological preference for the period, similar strategies seem to be closer to Mark Fisher's take on nostalgia as "a formal attachment to the techniques and formulas of the past, [which constitute] a consequence of a retreat from the modernist challenge of innovating cultural forms adequate to contemporary experience".[3] This might suggest that, in contrast to the academically infested Victoriana, the eighteenth century offers a different possibility for retro fiction: perhaps a politically safer space for seemingly non-controversial enactment of the past.

What follows looks into the ongoing preoccupation with vicarious experience and instability of control over the meaning in language throughout the novel. It is argued that such aspects of historical fiction set in the eighteenth century can be seen as indicative of the contemporary struggles with the awareness of the mediated status of representing experience and thus with the problematic nature of any attempts at returning to the past.

Vicarious Pleasures

The novel's continuous concern with recording, narrating and reading makes experience one of the central themes of Irwin's work. Regardless of the intricacies of this complex aspect of our existence, the doubts about it are widespread: from its role in the cognitive processes or in acquiring knowledge (*tabula rasa*), through deliberations on its nature (positive or negative), immediacy or the very possibility of mediation, to the problematic links with the subject, not to mention that it seems to be apparently impossible to put down in words.[4] From ancient Greek philosophy to postmodern doubts and incredulities about language, the lasting problem with experience is that it "is frequently employed as a marker for what is so ineffable and individual (or specific to a particular group) that it cannot be rendered in conventionally communicative terms to those who lack it".[5] The impossibility to mediate experiences, especially those of madness or pleasure, were also of interest to such French poststructuralist thinkers as Roland Barthes or Michel Foucault, who found them useful in disrupting the systematising discourses of knowledge.

Nevertheless, it is not only in such liminal states as sickness or erotic encounters that experience's representation fails. Although a hope for the interlocutor's identification with our lot makes one's communication into an attempt at exchanging experiences or at giving an account of them, this process seems inherently flawed by the difficulty of speaking from what Georges Bataille aptly called *Inner Experience*.[6] Feelings of empathy seem also akin to reading and literature – much realist fiction is frequently based on the reader's identification with what is read[7] and, consequently, evokes forms of immersion or of "the vicarious", whose Latin root suggests "substitute" or "replacement".[8] Both may relate to forms of identification with the characters within the storyworld perhaps comparable to mechanisms operating in practices like reading or interacting with visual media.[9]

While reading may provide different degrees of identification and emotional investment, literature and media in general, in their representational nature, still remain worlds apart from the real thing. Experience is simply "taken to be a non-fungible commodity" as it can sometimes "become an end in itself" escaping any exchange principles, i.e. forms of recounting one's experience.[10] Its relationship to identity politics also acquires special importance because of the situatedness of a discursive authority: "Who, after all, would want to trade one's own experience of sex for an account of another's?"; not to mention representing particularities of experience of, for example, women, whites, or what Jay calls "silenced minorities".[11] Given the omnipresence of these issues in the discursive renderings of reality, disparate contemporary theoretical orientations ask questions about the cultural/ racial/ gender positioning of the text, its origins or the ideas it argues in favour or against and analyse the complex implications of various discursive practices and their entanglement in the objects they describe. From this perspective, rendering sexual encounters, in writing, poses further challenges connected with identification and immersion. Georges Bataille, an important influence on both Barthes and Foucault, notices this in the viewing of intimate situations. Exploring the proximity between the erotic and other liminal experiences, he "rules out the possibility of dispassionate observation" due to recognising a particular "contagion" effect:

> It has nothing to do with that of germ-carried diseases. The contagion in question is like that of yawning or of laughter. A yawn makes one yawn, repeated gusts of laughter make me want to laugh, and if sexual activity is witnessed it is capable of rousing desire. It may also inspire disgust. Or we might put it that sexual activity even if only shown by a hardly perceptible agitation or by clothes in disarray easily induces in a witness a feeling of participation (at least if physical beauty lends significance to an incongruity of appearance).[12]

Reading affects the audience in a similar way, especially as the words on the page seem to appeal to one's imagination at least as effectively as images do in visual material. Correspondingly, it is these participatory qualities of fiction that were recognised and willingly explored in their eighteenth-century variations already in the early days of the novel as a genre. Simultaneously, such vicarious aspects were quickly fenced off as dangerous and corrupting, with the literature depicting vagaries of life or exploring libertine morality being especially controversial because of the graphic (or visual) renderings of carnal encounters and moral transgressions. Although verbal descriptions of the throes of passion were effectively exploring individual liberties of the time,[13] they were also visibly going against the grain of the period's dominant dictum of education and entertainment.

The debates about the potentially corrupting influence of literature stemmed from the very flexibility of narrative prose and from the vicarious qualities of the novel. From the very outset, it offered a space for probing the era's zeitgeist and for recording experiences. Although many of the founding authors at the time, like Defoe, Fielding or Voltaire, aimed to develop an image of contemporaneous society and its problems, their application of various popular modes was also connected to narrating aspects of experience.[14] Other English and French writers explored a wide scope of structuring options and narrative positioning (in travel writing, memoir or the letter form), often resorting to descriptions of someone's life.[15]

Indeed, experience was oozing out of writing in both content and form, especially in terms of (auto)biography and the epistolary novel. The former allowed for readerly identification, while the latter provided useful ways of recording experience. From this perspective, the determination exhibited by Jean-Jacques Rousseau in his *Confessions* to give a sincere account of his failings and achievements – including masturbatory practices and nocturnal intellectual activity – not only borders on a deliberate self-display through a first-person narration but can be connected with demonstrating how a narrative encapsulates one's consciousness in writing. Works like Goethe's *The Sorrows of Young Werther* (1774), Richardson's *Pamela* (1740) and *Clarissa* (1748), apart from being stories of individuals, also encourage identification with the protagonist.[16] Owing to its affinity with the communication practice in vogue at the time, the epistolary novel developed quickly in the Enlightenment. It was accompanied by a widespread presence of letters in virtually any domain – from politics, through religion, to philosophy or personal exchanges. Not limited to an informative function, letter writing became an outlet for expressing feelings and worldviews suggesting a positive evaluation of the very act of exploring affections. This tied in with fellow-feeling and honesty becoming philosophical and psychological terms with social and political implications in the eighteenth century in England and France.[17] Such a mixture of heart and reason appeared to merge individual aspirations, social mores and writing, with the double function of letters (obligations and pleasure) reflected in literature. Capable of containing fragments which originated in feelings or imagination but also in rational analyses, letters were employed in fiction to combine narrative discourse and various degrees of moralising, making the genre fit very well into the eighteenth-century aesthetic axioms of instruction and amusement. Perhaps that is also why in Georgian England the reading public resonated powerfully both to the pages of the *Spectator* (1711–1712) and to Richardson's *Pamela* or Frances Burney's *Evelina* (1778), novels "which granted readers the privilege of examining letters that their protagonists had read", leading

> on to the strikingly different narratives of genteel manners and historical adventure produced by Austen and Scott, in which exposure to texts again shaped pliant personalities like Fanny Price in *Mansfield Park* (1814), Catherine Morland in *Northanger Abbey* (1818) and the eponymous hero of *Waverley* (1814), the act of reading and its impact were unmistakable preoccupations not only for leading writers but also for the reading public.[18]

By 1778, the epistolary novel had already become "a thriving, indeed blooming, product circulating in the reading world with great success and especially prized for its much-vaunted unselfconsciousness";[19] so much so that other works using a similar mode to recount their plot were very often written in an intertextual correspondence with the mid-eighteenth-century heavyweights like *Clarissa* or *Sir Charles Grandson* (1753–1754) – they produced "a community of mutual readers and writers variously privy to the different parts of the correspondence circulating among them".[20] Comparatively free of formal constraints, the epistolary novel became a vehicle for the era's didacticism also because the open secret of the times was that letters, even if addressed to one recipient, would end up reaching a wider audience.[21]

Linked to the spontaneity of inspiration and the possibility of exchanging thoughts, letter writing fed on the relativity of points of view and on human curiosity allowing writers to problematise further boundaries of the personal and the public or the moral and the indecent. Philosophers wanting to prod their audiences into rethinking most radical ideas would also use the plasticity of the novel.[22] This is especially visible in the writings by Marquis de Sade or in the descriptions of the perverted aristocracy in Pierre Choderlos de Laclos' *Dangerous Liaisons* (1782).

In the Enlightenment, the term libertinism connoted the morally problematic feats believed to lead people away from the straight and narrow onto the demoralised path of lechery and lustfulness. Although the roots of such a conduct go back to antiquity's forms of self-awareness, with time they became connected to disparate understanding of individual liberties (e.g. Machiavelli). This becomes more complex in the British setting, especially in the light of public display of hedonism following the times of Charles II.[23] General references to libertine culture on the continent point to "the sexually free behaviour and norms of upper-class men, and in particular, of the French aristocracy during the decline of the ancien régime, as well as the writing which celebrates it", with examples from authors like Crébillon fils, Duclos, Diderot, Prévost and Laclos.[24] If libertinism in France opposed forms of dogmatism, e.g. the one represented by the church, and linked both to hedonism and dissident behaviours, the British polarity operated slightly differently: "the libertinism of the Cavalier Court was a salutary reminder of how hedonism not only destroyed itself through the bottle, pox or pistol, but also meant sinister alliances with Popish tyranny".[25] Similarly, with the Albion version of progress as individual improvement, "Kantian categorical imperatives found their English counterparts in a hedonic calculus".[26] Regardless of the cultural setting however, libertinism in everyday life was believed to result from conceptualising human activity as political and intellectual, with the term commonly employed as a pejorative label to discredit any transgressions against morality and conventional looseness, or in debates surrounding literary depictions of sex and sexuality. Today's French use of the term towards a lustful lecher blindly following his urges is based on past meanings indicating a hedonistic and sceptical disbeliever who would not flinch to feed his appetites for refined sexual pleasures; a stranger to feelings of remorse whose intensity of experiences was often reinforced by sexual pleasures, enhanced only when coupled with a performative display of disrespect towards the dominant mores, purity or self-restraint.

Owing to their interest in depravation, it is easy to see the libertine-like novels as anything but edifying and instructive. This, however, was not completely the case. The literary libertinism signified an unrestrained sexual desire juxtaposed or in negotiation with the conventionalities of morals, religion and civil codes – "a freedom available to an educated, often titled elite", which, with the discursive and philosophically informed practices of sexual freedom, merged "into libertinage – the vernacular, dissident freedoms of everyday life".[27] Moreover, this writing fitted particularly well with the stereotypical representations of female characters (pure and passive) dominating cultural texts at the time.[28] Perhaps owing to their pornographic elements,[29] many works of that kind were also associated with the fringes of mainstream literary production, but even here one finds a reliance on the biographic mode and experience recording techniques. Texts like *The School of Venus* (1680), *Venus in the Cloister* (1725), or *A Dialogue Between a Married Lady and a Maid* (1740), in addition to their marginal associations were suffused with a particular agenda concerning carnal experiences, pleasure and intellectual reflection.[30] As Kathleen Lubey identifies, one of the purposes of merging thinking, self-knowledge and bodily pleasures in literature tackling such experiences ("passion, love, prostitution, courtship, marriage") was to fuse erotic energies with the knowledge of the self and a socially acknowledged behaviour. Such writing thus served a paradoxically edifying purpose of probing the limits of individual self-control and morality where eroticism could be understood as a negotiation of desire and self-command, filtered through a diverse spectrum of sexual representation so that the resulting sexual arousal derived from reading would ultimately become a subject for contemplation.[31] In this sense, it would be wrong to assume solely questionable purposes. Although the pleasures of such reading come "from some combination of imagining others' libidinal arousals and, perhaps, feeling similar stirrings in one's own body",[32] the audience was to undergo a form cathartic cleansing and to be reinstated in society but with an understanding of self-determination within broader social context.

It seems that to some extent the popularity of the eighteenth-century epistolary novel stems from the possibility of readerly identification and from the controversies surrounding its libertine varieties. Although didactically problematic, the immersive potential of novels, even eroticised ones, can be recognised as part of a powerful engine in the eighteenth-century struggle between an emergent middle-class discourse of moral reformation and an older aristocratic "libertine" code.[33] Interestingly, very little was done to mask such an agenda. *Pamela*, for example, the novel about pious female social conduct in the face of inappropriate male advances, commences its didacticism already in the prefatory matter, as an announcement of the purpose to "divert", "entertain", "to instruct and improve the minds of youth of both sexes".[34] The self-examination of the eponymous heroine uses a letters and diary form which the reader is to follow – a practice rooted in the excitement of peeping into the private sphere of life but also in the religiously motivated intention to record and reflect on one's life. In securing a firm footing for the exploration of issues of privacy and self-examination, the eighteenth-century novel, in diary-keeping or autobiographical writing, performed at least a double function: recording consciousness and enabling vicarious participation in specific experiences. With charges of licentiousness in the air, such politically sensitive texts had to employ moralising to keep up the appearances of demonstrating the intrigue as subject to moral analysis.

A Blind Man's Rainbow

As time went by, eighteenth-century novels garnered a specific reputation which even the fictional readers were quick to recognise. It is the stereotypical content of such literature that one can see satirised, for example, in David Lodge's *Small World*:

> They're just debased versions of the sentimental novel of courtship and marriage that started with Richardson's *Pamela*. A realistic setting, an ordinary heroine that the reader can identify with, a simple plot about finding a husband, endless worrying about how far you should go with a man before marriage. Titillating but moral.[35]

Michel Irwin's *The Skull and the Nightingale* uses a similarly realistic setting of 1760s London and Worcestershire to explore aspects of libertinism within a part-epistolary, part-diary novel. Consequently, it resembles a piece both set and written in the eighteenth century, with the traces of its contemporary origins securely masked within a historicised simulacrum. Echoing *Tom Jones* and *Dangerous Liaisons*, especially because of the elaborate plotting and an emphasis on seduction and manipulation, the novel's multi-layered intertextuality suggests a peculiar filtering of the contemporary approach to literature.

Narrated by Richard Fenwick, a handsome 23-year-old who returns to London after a Grand Tour, the story traces the consequences of the "precarious position"[36] offered to the young man by his wealthy and powerful uncle, James Gilbert. Once liberated from the necessities of striving towards some productive end in life, Fenwick is allowed to live a life of pleasure because his aged godfather, after years of emotional self-restraint, wants to explore various passions: "Vanity, Greed, Avarice, Rage, Lust" (97). The reader thus tracks the gradual unfolding of flirtations, amorous conquests and morally corrupt dealings the protagonist is to execute. Drawing on a Faustian-like plot, Fenwick is allowed to savour diverse experiences only to grow more and more aware of the complex web of dependencies he had become part of. After falling in love again with his former sweetheart, Sarah Ogden, the familiar motifs of danger, betrayal and tragedy are subsequently enacted, much to the reader's surprise at their resolution. Correspondingly well-known are strategies typical of many historical novels in which "the real figures of the past are deployed to validate or authenticate the fictional world by their presence"; yet here they do not act to mask the stitches between history and fiction in "a formal and ontological sleight of hand".[37] Instead, the historicity of the text: a character has had his "features recorded by the ingenious Mr Hogarth" (108), Gilbert allegedly "dined with Walpole" (303), while others declare an intertextual awareness – "*Will that at last amount to merely a roguish chapter in* Peregrine Pickle *or to a whole novel by Mr Richardson?*" (252).

Avoiding any outward postmodern self-reflexivity, the novel thematises vicarious experience to act out its present-day origins, especially at the level of conceptualising the questions of control over meaning in language. Becoming a stand-in for the sinister uncle, Fenwick also positions the reader as an addressee of the narrator-participant explorations of the storyworld and the licentious dealings described in the text. Indeed, considerable effort is put into conjuring up various more or less stereotypical aspects of the Age of Enlightenment – from imitating the language, manners and intellectual discussions of the time to the obligatory place- and name-dropping (Hogarth, Johnson, Spence, Brown, etc.), including the lively coffee house debates and drunken male brawls. The meticulous research behind this work supplies an authenticating framework of progress and empiricist scrutiny, so that the characters can perceive the world around them as fresh and young, with "a million possibilities still unexplored" (23). Similarly, Fenwick at the outset of the narrative regards his face in the mirror as "a *tabula rasa*, awaiting the imprint of further experiences" (10).

Importantly, this unencumbered position which changes with time is also the one reserved for the audience, partly because of the very nature of the reading process and due to the focalisation employed in the text. The letter form of much of the novel supplemented by first-person diary-like accounts allows the flow of information between the characters to be traced and contributes to exposing the very vagaries of committing experience (events, feelings, sensations, etc.) to the medium of writing. While the letters serve to recount events, thus opening the possibility for vicarious participation, they also reveal the fragmented, unstable signification stemming from the limited point of view and from the very form of written interaction. That is why, as the story progresses, Fenwick desperately wants to remain in control over the meaning which his writing projects to the addressees: his uncle, friends, lovers and, ultimately, the reader. Taking the time to rewrite and edit the letters to his patron, he pays great attention to details and ponders on what he actually wants to communicate and remembers to preserve "fragmentary drafts of [his] earlier epistles" or to keep an archive to aid his official memory (81–82). The understanding of experience is thus plagued by a concern about this notion's problematic (ir)representability, not least about the potential for embodying contrasting meanings: "Who could describe a rainbow to a blind man? Worse, the very attempt at description would sully the thing described" (295). In initially outlining his agenda, Gilbert uses letters to speak about his intention of vicarious participation in life as seen "through younger eyes and experienced by livelier senses" (33). However, dominating the descriptions of his past fastidious life is an acceptance of the phantasmatic dimension of reading: "As a young man I found myself plagued – the word is not too strong – by the pastoral. Art, poetry, drama insisted that love should be idyllic, Arcadian. The reality fell short. The physical encounter could not match the rhetoric" (98). The interest in what he terms as rhetoric suggests both an awareness of the artificiality (i.e. mediated status) of representation and the gap between the imaginary and the real. As a result, Gilbert does not so much need the actual experiences themselves – he has already lived through some of them ("I found the din and the stench [of London] repellent and the social life artificial" [33]). Instead, what he craves is precisely the phantasmatic dimension provided by the very account of such events. Symptomatically, the mediated status of representation is not criticised for a lack of verisimilitude but valued positively, despite perhaps being at odds with reality. By extension, such valorisation can also be applied to fiction writing.

Implicated in such story-making are questions of discursive power and control, especially when it comes to the actually participating proxy. In this sense, the character of Gilbert resembles the figure of a solitary sage who had retreated from the world to live in isolation exercising speculative detachment from the world and people. Gradually, however, for both Fenwick and the reader, he is revealed as a wicked and lecherous old libertine holding his neighbours in debt, pursuing more and more depravity to secure command over everyone and everything around him. Even though his aims might partly correspond to Enlightenment thinking of "criticism and change", the process of achieving them is unethical – he is neither "the pedant, cooped up in a college, or the 'dull and deep potations' don", nor "an urban, sociable sort, in the vanguard of humanity, in touch with the people" for whom he could speak and write as an essayist or an itinerant scientific lecturer.[38] The pleasure he gains from vicarious participation does not result directly from filling in the void created by the mediated nature of communication or from the very act of consuming (i.e. reading) the more or less vivid descriptions of sexual encounters, but more from orchestrating such experiences. Aware of being in the position of power and control over their actors, Fenwick's Godfather declares to be in need of assistance when out for new sensations ("Without leaving my comfortable country estate I look forward to being escorted to regions of my experience that I could never have visited on my own" [67]) and recognises the secondary nature of such mediated participation ("I read still, and read eagerly, but I feel that I am cut off, like one in prison, from the life that books reveal and the life you now inhabit" [115]). Consequently, when Richard is guided to another act of seduction during one of his stays in the country, Gilbert is happy with limiting himself to spying on the tryst through a hole in the wall, as if keeping in line with his role of a tacit participant, "an unseen fellow traveller" [115]. The recounted exploits almost always overlap with a power struggle in which the erotic excitement comes from a sense of command and dominance. Consequently, the economy of desire between the characters is conceptualised by means of access to knowledge or a recognition that certain experiences remain otherwise unavailable. When Fenwick observes that the husband of the woman he obsesses over is privy to intimate experiences shared by the married couple and blocked from him, he complains that "this dull merchant had seen what I had not seen and been where I had not been" (114). Notably, he is not worried about ownership but about experience. Freed from the controlling gaze or from the necessity of giving an account of it, he is truly liberated only when he manages to have sex outdoors realizing that he does not have to report this event to his patron (217–218). Although such experiences may be shunned by some of the characters in the diegetic world, the reader still witnesses their discursive representation.

It is through such aspects of recording and representing experience that the novel marks its contemporary provenance. This is manifested in a modern awareness of the consequences of Enlightenment thinking and in asserting the text's simulated status, rather than through problematising its fictive quality, as would be typical of high postmodern fiction and the likes of Fowles or Vonnegut. The opening dictum, taken from Richardson's *Clarissa* ("There is no difference to be found between the skull of King Phillip and that of another man"), certainly indicates an understanding of the text's existence in relation to other works. Nevertheless, on a content level, this suggestion about a uniform physical nature shared by people is not solely an intertextual reference. Despite the contemporary tainting with relativity or discursive situatedness, Irwin's novel puts forth to the reader a historicised simulacrum which problematises the nature of historical knowledge in a way which is different from forms of historiographic metafiction.[39] In its original context, the quote from *Clarissa* functions as a dismissal of actual sexual experience. Richardson's text has the libertine Lovelace expressively indicate the physical similitude of the protagonist to other women so as to repudiate the account of what could only be classified as rape. The skull, originally referred to in a sexual context, in Irwin's book title is coupled with the nightingale to allude to the intellectual experiment discussed by the characters. When Fenwick and his friend stumble upon a man from a conversation club, he informs them:

> We returned to your theme and considered the case of the nightingale. Anatomize the bird and you will find lungs and membranes. There is the instrument, but where's the song? And where is the composer?' "You have killed him", cried Cullen, "for the sake of your experiment".
>
> (74)

Cullen's answer marks the modern understanding of the fleeting nature of the immateriality of experience and points to how it might be fatally destroyed by the scrutinising attempts to demystify and explain the matters of life. The characters thus express a contemporary grasp of the potential costs of the solely rational, scientific inquiry – the death of the subject in the course of scientific research. This also goes beyond the recognition of how "the eighteenth-century concern for lies and falsity becomes a postmodern concern for the multiplicity and dispersion of truth(s), truth(s) relative to the specificity of place and culture",[40] but echoes Adorno and Horkheimer's criticism of Enlightenment "instrumental reason" with its subjugating tendencies towards the world and knowledge detached from the ethical values.[41]

Couched in imitative poetics, the self-awareness of the narrative and its diegetic world's textual constructedness remains largely hidden under the authenticating veneer of intertextual references. Nevertheless, the unease about these matters informs references to the character life's fictive status, especially when Fenwick refers to a sense of "inhabiting two distinct narratives" (132, 248). As the shifting perspective of reporting is imbricated in a plurality of versions of truth resulting from different motivations and the correspondingly differing communicative arrangements, it is problematised in turn by the medium of letters and writing. If postmodern historiographic metafiction relied on what Hutcheon termed as an "unresolved contradiction",[42] Irwin's novel, on a very basic level, seems paradoxically intent on revelling in the past. Because the novel does not simply present immoral content (manipulation, sexual exploits, rape) for a more or less outwardly stated didactic purpose, it is the text's exploration of the relationship between reading and writing and the very phantasmatic power of immersive and vicarious qualities of literature that underlie the narrative. This is visible in the suggestion that vicarious experience can be enjoyed to the fullest precisely by means of an intermediary – a detached observer, or perhaps the reader. Moreover, the safety buffer of a proxy to report the events is connected to a present-day awareness of the mediated status of communication. The reader thus witnesses an eighteenth-century reader (Gilbert) interested in the non-fictive stories and events, but who, simultaneously, embraces their phantasmatic status, while being well aware of the textually constructed elements in such discursive practices. This is an awareness which Hutcheon identifies as postmodern. On another level, present-day readers may see in Gilbert a metaphor of themselves, perfectly mindful of the fact that they are, both, reading a "fake" narrative which attempts to pass off as an eighteenth-century text, and who are still capable of enjoying the immersive and vicarious qualities that come with it, despite their rather mellow political impact.

Conclusion

As a textual construct, literature provides occasions for recording experience and possibilities of vicarious identification with the characters and their stories. This immersive potential of fiction became particularly strongly pronounced with eighteenth-century libertine fiction which met with critical voices precisely because of being identified as morally dubious and titillating. Despite negative stereotypes, such novels served as instruments of developing self-awareness and could play an active role in fostering self-governing in line with the period's educational bent. In this sense, the political significance of such writing rested in teasing out the dominant morality which could be channelled into something socially useful. Recent academic interest in the understanding of the constructed character of historical narratives points to the situatedness of any discursive revisiting of the past and resulted in the studies of such politically sensitive issues as the role of women in such representations[43] or the practical dimensions of theory with respect to historical fiction, among others.[44]

Irwin's book replicates the erstwhile genre of the epistolary novel but without an awareness of this context or a tangible political tooth of the controversial eighteenth-century works. Written in an impeccable yet anachronistic style, the novel employs period poetics originating from sound research. However, it seems to concentrate its textual energies more on stylistic prefigurations – possibly to disavow its contemporary origins or perhaps to escape the debate around identity politics and other controversial issues. Its insistence on explorations of vicarious experience demonstrates the text's present-day status and an involvement in the phantasmatic pleasures offered by literature in general. The text's very construction, in which the reader witnesses accounts of layered experiences, enacts a particular model for the consumption of writing – one where the reader views it as a record of experiences while remaining seemingly removed from the storyworld.

What may be seen as problematic about such literary simulations is their deliberate self-enclosure ultimately devoid of political involvement. While the choice of a first-person perspective and an epistolary/ diary form questions narrative credibility, such positioning of the writer, reader and the text also sets up the possibility of an engaged, vicarious participation. This, in turn, reveals instabilities behind any attempts at textual control over meaning, also affected by the contemporary recognition of the constructed status of representations. Having identified genuine experience as informing the stories in the diegetic world, such narratives become more attractive for the domineering uncle and, consequently, for the reader. Their insistence on a solely expository quality points to their aesthetic purpose and since they are not questioned, parodied or commented on critically, the present-day audience is encouraged to view such historical fiction "merely" as a "pleasure read", with the feeling resulting from an escapist involvement in reading. It may well be that the lack of any outward political expectations in such seemingly unencumbered historical fiction is actually part of its allure.

Notes

1   See Kym Brindle, *Epistolary Encounters in Neo-Victorian Fiction: Diaries and Letters* (Houndmills: Palgrave Macmillan, 2013).
2   See Fredric Jameson, *Postmodernism, or, the Cultural Logic of Late Capitalism* (London and New York: Verso, 2008), 19–25.
3   Mark Fisher, *Ghosts of My Life: Writings on Depression, Hauntology and Lost Futures* (Winchester and Washington: Zero Books, 2014, kindle edition), not paginated.
4   See Martin Jay, *Songs of Experience: Modern American and European Variations on a Universal Theme* (Berkeley: University of California Press, 2005).
5   Jay, *Songs of Experience*, 5.
6   Georges Bataille, *Inner Experience*, trans. Leslie Anne Boldt (Albany: State University of New York Press, 1988).

7 See Marylin Charles, *The Stories we Live: Psychoanalysis and Literature* (Lanham: Rowman & Littlefield, 2015).

8 Alain Berhoz, *The Vicarious Brain, Creator of Worlds*, trans. Giselle Weiss (Cambridge, MA and London: Harvard University Press, 2017), 5.

9 This is due not only to the narrative nature of the latter's many forms (including interactive ones), but also through offering mediated (vicarious) experiences for their audience. The avatars of these might be called "virtual vicars" (see Berhoz, *The Vicarious Brain,* 7–8).

10 Jay, *Songs of Experience*, 6.

11 Jay, *Songs of Experience*, 6.

12 Georges Bataille, *Death and Sensuality: Eroticism and Taboo*, trans. Mary Dalwood (New York: Walker and Company, 1962), 152.

13 See Peter Cryle and Lisa O'Connel (eds.), *Libertine Enlightenment: Sex, Liberty and License in the Eighteenth Century* (Houndmills: Palgrave Macmillan, 2003); or Marine Ganofsky, *Night in French Libertine Fiction* (Oxford: Voltaire Foundation, 2018).

14 Pierre Malandain, "Panorama Europy (Pierwsza połowa XVIII wieku. Oświecenie)", in *Literatura Europy. Historia Literatury Europejskiej*, ed. Annick Benoit-Dusausoy and Guy Fontaine, trans. Elżbieta Skibińska et al. (Gdańsk: słowo/obraz terytoria, 2009), 444.

15 Malandain, "Panorama Europy", 446.

16 See Uta Janssens-Knorsch and Hans-Christof Graf von Nayhauss, "Panorama Europy (Druga połowa XVIII wieku)", in *Literatura Europy. Historia Literatury Europejskiej*, ed. Annick Benoit-Dusausoy and Guy Fontaine, trans. Elżbieta Skibińska et al. (Gdańsk: słowo/obraz terytoria, 2009), 488.

17 See Janssens-Knorsch, von Nayhauss, "Panorama Europy", 488.

18 David Allan, *Commonplace Books and Reading in Georgian England* (Cambridge: Cambridge University Press, 2010), 10.

19 Ros Ballaster, "The Rise and Decline of the Epistolary Novel, 1770-1832", in *The Oxford Handbook of The Eighteenth-Century Novel*, ed. J.A. Downie (Oxford: Oxford University Press, 2016), 409.

20 Ballaster, "The Rise and Decline of the Epistolary Novel", 414.

21 Abigail Williams, *The Social Life of Books: Reading Together in the Eighteenth-Century Home* (New Haven and London: Yale University Press, 2017).

22 Malandain, "Panorama Europy", 446.

23 See Jeremy W. Webster, *Performing Libertinism in Charles II's Court: Politics, Drama, Sexuality* (Houndmills: Palgrave Macmillan, 2005).

24 Peter Cryle and Lisa O'Connel, "Sex Liberty and Licence in the Eighteenth Century", in *Libertine Enlightenment*, 2.

25 Roy Porter, *Enlightenment: Britain and the Creation of the Modern World* (London: Penguin Books, 2001, Apple books edition), 84.

26 Porter, *Enlightenment*, 1044.

27 Cryle and O'Connel, "Sex Liberty and Licence in the Eighteenth Century", 2.

28 A. D. Harvey, *Sex in Georgian England* (London: Phoenix, 2001).
29 W. Kendrick argued in favour of viewing pornography as distinctly modern discourse, appearing only at the turn of the eighteenth century. The OED notes it to be "an early nineteenth-century neologism" with etymology in "whore writing" or "writing by or about whores"; correspondingly, this modern category may be thus problematic in terms of its application towards works classified as pornographic when this category did not exist (qtd. in Bradford K. Mudge (ed.), *When Flesh Becomes Word: An Anthology of Early Eighteenth-Century Libertine Literature* (Oxford: Oxford University Press, 2004), xxiv.
30 See Mudge (ed.), *When Flesh Becomes Word.*
31 Kathleen Lubey, *Excitable Imaginations. Eroticism and Reading in Britain, 1660-1760* (Lewisburg: Bucknell University Press, 2012), 3 *et passim.*
32 Lubey, *Excitable Imaginations*, 13.
33 Jonathan Mee, "Libertines and Radicals in the 1790s: The Strange Case of Charles Pigott I", in *Libertine Enlightenment*, 185.
34 Samuel Richardson, *Pamela, or, Virtue Rewarded* (1740; London: Cock and McGowan, 1816), iii.
35 David Lodge, *Small World: An Academic Romance* (London: Penguin Books, 1985), 258.
36 Michael Irwin, *The Skull and the Nightingale* (London: Blue Door, 2013), 25. Further references to Irwin's novel will be parenthetical.
37 Linda Hutcheon, *The Poetics of Postmodernism: History, Theory, Fiction* (New York and London: Routledge, 2004), 114. Hutcheon is referring to the theory of György Lukács.
38 Porter, *Enlightenment*, 1017.
39 See Hutcheon, *The Poetics of Postmodernism*, esp. 105–123.
40 Hutcheon, *The Poetics of Postmodernism*, 108.
41 See Max Horkheimer and Theodor W. Adorno, *Dialectic of Enlightenment: Philosophical Fragments*, ed. Gunzelin Schmid Noer, trans. Edmund Jephcott (1944; Stanford: Stanford University Press, 2002).
42 Historiographic metafiction "keeps distinct its formal auto-representation and its historical-context, and in so doing problematizes the very possibility of historical-knowledge, because there is no reconciliation, no dialectic here—just *unresolved contradiction*" (Hutcheon, *The Poetics of Postmodernism*, 106; my emphasis).
43 See Ros Ballaster, *Seductive Forms: Women's Amatory Fiction from 1684 to 1740* (Oxford: Oxford University Press, 2007).
44 See Brindle, *Epistolary Encounters in Neo-Victorian Fiction.*

6   Renarrating Women's Stories
Imogen Hermes Gowar's *The Mermaid and Mrs. Hancock*

Joanna Maciulewicz

The Mermaid and Mrs. Hancock, a 2018 magical realist novel by Imogen Hermes Gowar, seems a particularly good example of neo-historical fiction, since it overcomes the dissociation of "the self-reflexive" and "its traditionally accepted contrary – the historico-political context in which it is embedded", characteristic of historiographic metafiction.[1] The author of the novel, having studied historical artefacts and documents from the eighteenth century, scrupulously recreates the realities of life in the Georgian period without renouncing an interest in the problems of the representation of the past. The realism of her depiction of the eighteenth century cannot be viewed, however, as a simple revival of Sir Walter Scott's original model of historical fiction, which is believed to have paved the way to Victorian realist writing. After Roland Barthes demonstrated that realism relies on "conformity […] to the cultural rules of representation" rather than on fidelity to the external reality,[2] there is no return to a straightforward, innocent verisimilitude. Gowar's novel is rather an example of the new way the representation of the past is problematised in the contemporary historical novel, in which, as Elodie Rousselot explains, the "critical engagement with that past may appear to be absent, while it is in fact seamlessly embedded into the fabric of the text".[3] The critical strand in Gowar's novel manifests itself in the evocation of themes and modes of writing characteristic of the forms of fiction that were ousted from the novelistic tradition and that have been retrieved from literary history only in recent studies of eighteenth-century creative writing.

The focus of *The Mermaid and Mrs. Hancock* is on the sex trade, an aspect of Georgian life that was rarely placed in the centre of attention of eighteenth-century canonical fiction. Gowar describes it as a logical extension of social life shaped by the logic of commerce, rather than its negative reflection. The manner of its description is characterised

by the combination of realism and fantasy. Having studied biographical texts, court transcripts and other historical documents, *Harris's
List* or *Nocturnal Revels* among them, Gowar scrupulously recreates
the material reality of the Georgian period, its food, clothes, architecture, and human sensory experiences of the world. The borders of
empirical realism, however, are pushed to include the marvellous. The
author introduces the motif of a mermaid, which becomes a pretext
for the exploration of the proximity of science and imagination in
the Enlightenment, and an opportunity to assume a more metaphorical way of describing reality, peculiar to nonrealist styles of writing.
The use of the marvellous helps portray the predicament of women,
who, having lost the support of traditional social institutions, recourse
to commodifying their bodies to make their fortune in the world
regulated by the rules of the market. In an interview, Gowar explains
that mermaids "were aligned very closely in the cultural imagination
with unchecked female sexuality, and that for the Georgians was
frightening".[4] The motif of mermaids creates an opportunity to bring
to light subjects and conventions that had been pushed to the margins
of novelistic tradition.

The Mermaid and Mrs. Hancock engages then with what G.S.
Rousseau and Roy Porter termed the "underbelly of the European
Enlightenment", that is, "that large and often amorphous bulk of
ideas and patterns of behaviour that thrives on the unaccountable, the
anomalous, the exotic".[5] In literature, these ideas assumed forms that
eluded easy classifications and that developed, as Srinivas Aravamudan
put it, "outside the Whiggish 'rise of the novel' that tells a very selective
story about fictional genres".[6] One example of the literary underbelly
is the kind of writing that Aravamudan dubbed as "Enlightenment
Orientalism", a body of transnational fiction, including a wide array
of forms – allegory, realism, satire, fantasy among them – that explores
significant philosophical issues from an intercultural perspective.
Another type of fiction that embraced the ideas developing outside
of the Enlightenment mainstream were pornographic and prostitute
narratives that functioned until recently as a "great wastebin of the
nonliterary".[7]

Gowar's creative endeavour to tap into the noncanonical fiction of
the Georgian period in an attempt to uncover the motifs relegated to the
cultural underworld corresponds to recent developments in the critical
study of eighteenth-century literature. The availability of digital research
tools, such as electronic catalogues and online databases, has made it
possible to access and to study numerous texts from outside of the still
relatively narrow canon and to gain a much greater awareness of the

diversity of the modes of writing created by eighteenth-century writers trying their luck in the rapidly expanding print market. The retrieval of the themes, conventions, and genres that had fallen into oblivion gives us a better – that is, broader and more complex – view of the eighteenth-century world and the diverse ways in which it was described, but it also brings to light what William Warner in his 1998 study calls "the violence of cultural memory"[8] that shapes literary history. Warner argues that it transforms "the strife of history into a repertoire of forms [...] by taking differences that may have motivated the writing or reading of novels within specific historical contexts – differences of religion, politics, class, gender, social propriety, race, or ethical design – and converting them into differences of a literary kind".[9]

Literary historians from the eighteenth century until now, Warner continues, have in the majority understood their task as that of cultural valorisation. The dominant theory of the rise of the novel, which has discarded many fictional genres as the novel's "other" against which the legitimate genre could define itself, is the most relevant example. In contrast, more recent critical studies try to uncover the luxurious undergrowth of eighteenth-century fiction. Leah Orr, for instance, used online databases to read almost five hundred works of fiction printed between 1690 and 1730 "to achieve an understanding of the literature of the past that is more historically sensitive and comprehensive".[10] *Prose Fiction in English From the Origins of Print to 1750* (2017), a multi-author volume edited by Thomas Keymer, without attempting to "establish [...] a single unyielding narrative about [...] the complex and diffuse trends underlying the emergence of the novel in its modern form" surveys "the vital role of imported traditions, and the rich swirl throughout the period of many shifting, intermingling, and generically mutating narrative firms".[11] These studies seem to reverse the critical process of the refinement of the category of the novel that has led to its conceptualisation as a narrative "centralized around particular national culture, and reiterating parochial versions of domestic realism".[12]

In drawing themes from noncanonical fictional genres, such as prostitute narratives or fantastic tales, *The Mermaid and Mrs. Hancock* probes the nature of eighteenth-century modes of realism that were very different from Ian Watt's formal realism.[13] Watt, in his seminal *The Rise of the Novel* (1957), wrote that "the novelist's primary task is to convey the impression of fidelity to human experience"[14] by constructing plots that "had to be acted by particular people in particular circumstances".[15] He was very careful, however, to distinguish this kind of realism from the manner of representation characteristic of prenovelistic fictional forms, such as fabliaux or (Spanish) picaresque narratives, which focussed on low life and portrayed "life from the seamy side".[16] Sordid stories of criminals, beggars or prostitutes living on the margins of society seemed to him romances in reverse rather than true pictures of the world. Such a definition of novelistic realism echoes the eighteenth-century critical efforts to adjust fiction writing to the dominant epistemological, moral and aesthetic climate of the period.

A clear example of what happened to the texts that did not conform to the ideological premises of the emergent model of realism is the reception of John Cleland's *Memoirs of a Woman of Pleasure* (1748–1749), a novel that shares with *The Mermaid and Mrs. Hancock* a focus on the world of prostitution. The fact that it had remained not only a noncanonical but also "an underground book"[17] until the 1960s is the best testimony to the reductive forces of cultural memory. Although sex, as Roy Porter notes, was "a prominent part of [Enlightenment] written and printed culture",[18] the novel's allegiance to the bourgeois moral code made it impossible to address it in an open way. Today, Cleland's *Memoirs* enjoys the status of a novel. Paul Baines describes it as "culminating proof that the novel could be pornographic, and pornography, indeed, novelistic".[19] Peter Sabor, the editor of the Oxford World's Classics edition, declared in his introduction that it is "an important eighteenth-century novel, representing a significant development in English prose fiction"[20] that "differs from the mainstream of the eighteenth-century novel only in its explicit and obsessive interest in sexuality".[21]

The exclusion of Cleland's narrative from the novelistic tradition does not mean that novelists omitted the subject of prostitution altogether. Daniel Defoe's *Moll Flanders* and *Roxana* show that this is not the case. Defoe's realism, however, as is made evident in the preface to *Moll Flanders*, had self-imposed limitations, which *The Mermaid and Mrs. Hancock*, written in the twenty-first century, did not seem to need. The putative editor of the title character's account of her life as "a whore", "a thief" and "a transported felon in Virginia", confesses that her manuscript has been refined. "When a Woman debauch'd from her Youth [...] comes to give an Account of all her vicious Practises, and even to descend to the particular Occasions and Circumstances, by which she first became wicked, and of all the Progression of Crime", it is necessary to "put it into a Dress fit to be seen".[22] The editor's disclaimer is indicative of the attempts to adjust the descriptions of the "low life" to the aesthetic and moral purposes of fiction, which led to the editing of the language as well as the content of the text.

This description of the purification of the early novel of what was originally lewd or indecorous is one of many manifestations of how the social and discursive spaces of the bourgeois public sphere were conceptualised as "an 'idealist' realm of judgment, refinement, wit and rationalism" by "the suppression and distancing of the physical body".[23] The aim was to create "a sublimated public body without smells, without coarse laughter, without organs",[24] which were relegated to the realm of popular culture. This is not to say that corporeality was eliminated altogether. As is evident in Jonathan Swift's or Alexander Pope's texts, which frequently used scatology, the grotesque body was there but only to be disavowed and projected onto the aspects of life ousted from official culture. "It could never be owned"[25] as a legitimate part of bourgeois identity.

The focus of *The Mermaid and Mrs. Hancock* on the sexual underworld is justified by the ubiquity of prostitutes in the eighteenth-century world that could scarcely be overlooked or ignored. Markman Ellis and Ann Lewis say that they were "notoriously visible" and that "the scandal of prostitution" was the open defiance of "the established ideology of gender that championed a chaste and domestic femininity".[26] What is equally significant to bear in mind about the presence of the sex trade was that it was an integral part of eighteenth-century social life. Tony Henderson explains that, contrary to what might be thought,

[p]rostitutes were not [...] geographically separated from the mass of the city's population. Nor were they separated socially. They walked the same streets, they drank in the same public houses and gin shops, frequented the same parks, and in many cases lived in the same houses as Londoners of most, if not all, social classes.[27]

In many respects the underworld seemed like a natural extension of the respectable social life, frequently serving as its foil and the mirror image.

The ubiquity of prostitutes in London is dramatised in one of the scenes in *The Mermaid and Mrs. Hancock* in which Mr Hancock takes a night walk:

all along the Strand the girls are coming out for their evening's work: they perch on doorsteps and window ledges, or stand in small groups, passing a bottle between them and flirting their brightly coloured skirts up to show their frilled petticoats beneath.

(171–172)[28]

The observation of the women leads Mr Hancock to reflect upon the nature of the trade and its place in the commercial society of London.

> He sees printers' apprentices with their inky fingers, blacksmith's and pie-men and builders and lawyers. Doctors bustle in the streets in their cauliflower wigs; apothecaries scoop from great majolica jars; furniture salesmen sit happy behind mullioned windows. But amongst all this brave order there are those who have fallen loose from it, as screws from a fine machine. In this city of a thousand trades, there is only one that the women return to as if they were called to it.
>
> (174)

The streetwalkers whom Mr Hancock encounters during his walk represent only one category of sex traders in eighteenth-century society. Gowar's novel, however, presents a whole gallery of prostitutes, describing them with a flair comparable to *Harris's List of Covent Garden Ladies*, an almanac of prostitutes, published between 1757 and 1795, which, included details about their ages, addresses, prices and biographies.

In showing diverse experiences of women engaged in the sex trade, *The Mermaid and Mrs. Hancock* takes after prostitute narratives popular in the eighteenth century, which, as Laura J. Rosenthal notes, captured particularly well the "conflicting constructions and negotiations of personal identity in Britain's emergent commercial society".[29] By commodifying their own body and sexuality, sex traders embodied the ideal of possessive individualism that the new model of society promoted, taking it "to a logical conclusion",[30] while exposing the illusive "separation of the financial and the erotic", the public and private spheres, which the emergent bourgeois culture was striving to construct.[31] Unlike the eighteenth-century novels that presented prostitution as a "haunting alternative to domestic virtue",[32] prostitute narratives told the stories of women, who, deprived of the traditional safety nets of family or estate, turned to the sex trade for the means of support, and showed that "there was no foregone conclusion about how a prostitute's life would turn out".[33] The diversity of stories told by prostitute narratives, stories of success and stories of downfall and misery, "provides an enlightening context for the emphasis on female virtue in the novel"[34] and illustrates the divergent effects that the destabilization of traditional structures have on the predicament of women. Embracing the rules of the market by self-commodification may lead to financial advancement

and liberation from the constraints of class or gender roles or to degrad-
ation and objectification of one's self.

Like prostitute narratives, the many stories of sex traders included
in *The Mermaid and Mrs. Hancock*, some more developed, the others
in the form of mere vignettes, explore the options and the pitfalls that
the commercialisation of social life, and the flourishing marketplace
created for women. The story of Angelica Neal, a luxurious courtesan,
illustrates the promises of emancipation created for women willing to
and capable of commodifying their own sexuality to exploit the oppor-
tunities afforded by the sex trade, the illusion of the sense of liberty,
which the reliance on the market creates, and the inseparability of the
economy and private life. The beginning of her life story fits the convention: a sentimental narrative in which a girl, having lost the support of
her family, falls into prostitution. Angelica's father left his family destitute when he went to the colonies in the hope of making a fortune. This
is when she first learnt that "when you are a poor woman, and unpro-
tected, you are near as well a whore, even if you have not fallen yet"
(265). The continuation of Angelica's tale, however, demonstrates that
a loss of family protection and the enforced recourse to the market may
well awaken in women a spirit of entrepreneurship and create oppor-
tunities for them to shape their lives. Angelica Neal understood that her
"situation is a matter of economy" and resolved to see prostitution as a
chance of empowerment rather than as an embarrassing loss of virtue.
"What shall I be, all on my own, a poor woman who is ashamed of herself, or a rich one who is not?" (265), she says. The sex trade seems to her
"the secret otherworld of commerce in which she is as powerful as [the
men who desire her]" (135).

She cannot but learn that emancipation and empowerment in the sex
trade rest on shaky foundations when she chooses a lover for reasons
that are not mercenary. She enjoys a brief spell of contentment, when
her lover, unbound by any legal commitment, keeps her handsomely,
until his family, terrified by the dent that the cost of her keeping made
in the gentleman's fortune, puts a swift and easy close to her idyllic life.
The conclusion of the short-lived affair is a valuable lesson about the
precariousness of the sex trade and she proves to be a quick learner.
When Mr Hancock, an unattractive merchant enamoured with her,
offers to marry her, she embraces the opportunity and opts for a modest
life in a relationship in which she is protected by marriage laws.

The story of Polly, a black girl who works at Mrs Chappell's luxurious brothel, demonstrates that overconfidence in the marketplace's
ability to liberate a woman from the social constraints of gender, or

race, may lead to a much more bitter ending. Polly, like Angelica, hopes that in the "secret otherworld commerce" she can use her blackness as an asset and a source of power over men. At a party where she is sent by her keeper and employer Mrs Chappell, she is desired because she is exotic. "You are a woman entirely out of the common water; we all desire to sample every sort of woman there is in the world" (268), she hears from one of the men. She believes that her exoticism adds to her value and makes her the mistress of her fate. "I am not a toy to be passed about. I am an item of great value and rarity which few men are fortunate enough to ever possess. If you want me, you will earn me" (269), she declares with pride.

Polly believes that in the sex trade she can use her race as an asset that will liberate her from the fate of the other blacks of London who are poor and enslaved. When Angelica's lover refers to the black community as her brothers, she is "ruffled" by his words: "as if she had a single thing in common with the Africans and the indigent poor who clutter the streets" (238). She reacts in the same way to Mrs Chappell's footman's suggestion that she could leave the brothel and seek the protection of other blacks, her brothers, protesting against being considered as one of their kind. "'I've no brothers. I am not poor'" (249). It is only when she has decided to leave Mrs Chappell's house that she reconsiders her affinity with other Africans. The change of her predicament reveals to her that although the market in favourable circumstances may lead to emancipation, it may equally well reduce an individual to the dehumanising condition of a usable object that, ironically enough, is nothing short of slavery.

Polly's power over her own life and body is directly proportionate to the money she can generate. She thinks that her race makes her superior to other girls since men will pay more for her, but in fact "the men pay more [...] but fewer choose her" (238). The lower demand for her services translates into depreciation of her position in the brothel community, immediately exposing the state of dependence which the comfort of her life in Mrs Chappell's establishment effectively concealed. To illuminate this kind of dependence and the way it is experienced, Gowar resorts to scatology, which is to convey the sense of mortification that accompanies the loss of control over one's own body. In one scene, which faintly echoes a similar though much lighter, jocular incident described in Laurence Sterne's *A Sentimental Journey*, the bawd Chappell relieves herself in a carriage and chooses Polly to hold the newly filled chamber pot until the end of the ride. The prolonged description of the unsavoury situation serves as an objective correlative of the growing repugnance Polly feels as her senses are assaulted one after another. She sees Mrs

Chappell "heaving herself up so as to accommodate the vessel against her coarse and greying cauliflower". Then "the sound of her pissing fills the carriage" while "a mineral, creaturous smell [...] creeps into the nostrils". The chamber pot is passed to Polly and "its porcelain belly is hot against her palms". The girl holds it during the ride feeling "with each jolt of the carriage the abbess's piss slop and jump in its shallow vessel" while a "trickle escapes and tickles her finger" (236, 237). The ample details do not only serve to intensify the palpable realism of the scene but signify Polly's confrontation with her own powerless predicament.

She experiences the harshest effects of the commodification of her body after she has left the brothel and has to look for her customers on the street to support herself. An explicit account of one of the sexual acts that she has to suffer to pay for her daily needs, describing all the sordid aspects of the experience, reveals her abject powerlessness, her lack of agency, the objectification of her body and her extremely low market value. She can be used by the most despicable men who are ready to pay the six shillings she asks. One of her customer's "breath reeks so strongly of decay as if his mouth were a meat-safe that some sluttish housewife had abandoned a flitch of bacon within" (307). His clothes smell "of stagnant water and sour milk, gravy splattered from the crust of a pie, and his own dreadful odour, of an animal turning around and around in its own sweat and filth" (307). "He holds her so hard against the wall that she thinks he will do her mischief," but, in his brutality and indifference to her humanity, he prevents her from seeking a more comfortable position. After the act, "his leavings trickle down the inside of her thigh, warm at first but cold where the air begins to touch it" (308). She then "stops to mop herself with her petticoats" (308). The brutal use of her body, described in all graphic details, strips her of all the illusions of control over her life, and emphasises the ruthless objectification of her person to which self-commodification has led her.

The dirty realism of the scenes from the lives of London prostitutes is interspersed with descriptions of the marvellous, which provide a pretext to reflect on the role of wonder and imagination in eighteenth-century interest in scientific investigations and on the role of fantasy in novelistic discourse. The two mermaids that are introduced into the plot of *The Mermaid and Mrs. Hancock* have been brought to Mr Hancock by the captain of his ship from his voyages. The fact that they derive from the realm beyond the bounds of familiar reality forges a subtle connection with Oriental fiction, one of the novel's "underground generic cousins", and draws attention to the fact that fiction was conceptualised as "a kind of a fabricated import, a hybrid construction similar to other commodities in demand and imported from the Orient in the period, such as Indian muslin or Chinese porcelain".[35] The use of the marvellous can also be read as a reminder about the significant role of imagination, "wild fancies",[36] in the process of knowledge making, which had gradually diminished in the Enlightenment, as has been demonstrated recently by Tita Chico, who describes "disassociation of literariness from its epistemological sibling, science, as a source of truth about the natural and social worlds".[37] The relegation of fantasy from the realm of knowledge was followed by ousting it from the emerging novel, which defined itself against the genres using the marvellous. The readers were encouraged to search for "wonder in the everyday" rather than in the fantastic.[38] *The Mermaid and Mrs. Hancock*, like Oriental tales, uses the marvellous both to remind the reader that imagination plays a role in knowledge seeking, that "fiction's untruths [can] generate enlightenment"[39] about the world, and that this role of the marvellous has been obliterated from eighteenth-century epistemological and novelistic discourses.

The first of the two mermaids introduced in the novel is an example of "the exotic marvelous",[40] a type of zoological curiosity that is not interpreted by the implied audience, and by characters in the narrative, as the fantastic since it comes from the remote and unfamiliar regions of the world. The marvellous creature is brought to Mr Hancock by the captain of his ship from one of his trading voyages. The sensible merchant is scarcely pleased with his captain's decision, without first consulting him, to purchase the freak of nature, particularly when he learns that the captain had to sell his ship to be able to pay for the creature. Yet, he lets himself be persuaded that, at the time of a growing interest in the marvels of nature, the possession of a mermaid affords a rare opportunity to capitalise on the curiosity of London crowds. The story evokes the scientific fascination with the marvels of nature, which can be observed, for instance, in the Royal Society's instructions for the authors of travel reports, who were encouraged to observe "[a]ny thing [...] strange or remarkable among the Beasts, Birds, Insects, or Fishes"[41] and to record it in "a rhetoric of plain facts to safeguard against charges of romantic embellishments".[42]

The description of the wonder of which Mr Hancock found himself not-too-proud-an owner is accurate and unembellished and does not mitigate the hideousness of the creature for the reader who might have more romantic expectations of a mermaid. The narrator declares that the mermaid "is the size of an infant, and like an infant its ribcage is delicate and pathetic beneath its parchment skin, and its head is large, and its fists are drawn up to its face [...]. It has "fearful claws", "sharp fangs" a "torso [which] ends in the tail of a fish" (32). It is the most "dismaying oddity" (34) repugnant to its viewers. Despite its obviously marvellous nature, the mermaid seems so prosaic that Mrs Chappell, who hires it to revive the flagging interest in her brothel, decides to display it against a more attractive background and creates a mermaid's grotto for it. With the help of "an array of great glass fish tanks, with gilt chasing, full of green water and pearly fish" (125), few candles, silk and strings of pearls, Mrs Chappell created an illusion of an underwater world. The mermaid itself is exhibited on a plinth and is surrounded by coral. In the room there is a fountain and girls are singing. It seems that without a fantasy context the marvel is too inconspicuous to fulfil visitors' expectations.

The creature that defies classification of the species quite naturally awakens curiosity but it also opens the question of its authenticity. The viewers' frequently incredulous reactions to the marvel provide Gowar with a pretext to reflect on the inadequacies of empirical methods of enquiry and on science's dependence on the tales of travellers whose reports about marvellous, or merely exotic, creatures were difficult to verify. When Mr Hancock sees the mermaid for the first time, he suspects that it is a fake and looks for telltale signs of the way it was "done" but he is unable to discern stiches, glue or paint. Captain Jones assures him that the creature is a work of nature: "this is not *done*! It simply *is*" (33). A member of the Royal Society, "after hours of increasingly frantic scrutiny" (76), tries to protest against the mermaid's genuineness but his arguments are refuted. Science, as he is reminded, accepted the legitimacy of the unknown creatures on lesser evidence. The evidence of kangaroo, for one instance, was accepted on the basis of "a mere tanned hide" and the testimonies of Captain Cook and the members of his crew. The existence of mermaids, in contrast, is testified by the accounts of numerous sailors. "In annals [...] there is centuries worth of evidence to satisfactory account for the existence of sea-maidens, and yet none at all for what creatures may creep upon the plains of an entire body of land that nobody visits" (77). Travellers, scientists and fiction writers shared the thirst for wonder and direct observation could be insufficient to draw a definitive distinction between the natural and supernatural.

It is only the introduction of the second mermaid in *The Mermaid and Mrs. Hancock* that situates the novel more securely in the realm of the fantastic and demonstrates that the use of the marvellous may be as efficient a method of representing the truth about the reality as circumstantial descriptions of realist narratives. The second mermaid is a living creature captured by Captain Jones at the request of Mr Hancock, who wants to fulfil Angelica Neal's jocular wish for her own marvel. The way the narrator refers to it is very different from the way he described the first one. It remains elusive for the senses and it is only its supernatural influence on people that is palpable. The narrator never describes its appearance nor asserts its authenticity but merely reports on characters' observations. First, Captain Jones describes it in a letter informing Mr Hancock that his quest was successful and that the mermaid was caught alive. "Wonder of wonders", he writes, "[...] we came upon a true Mermaid. She had been caught up in the Nets of fishing-boat, which mistook her at first for a school of Herring, so vast and glinting was she. [...] She is very large and fine, and nothing indeed like you have ever seen in your life, and yet there is no mistaking what it is" (310). Then, there is an account of what Mr Hancock could discern in the vat in which the mermaid was kept. At first, he cannot make it out in the water at which he stares but then he sees her:

> She is indistinct but there is no doubting she is there. She is like a shoal of tiny fish, all surging and flickering together, a great mass that forms and re-forms and thinks all in accord. He can make out sometimes her arms, and often her swirling hair. He sees the silvery rolling-over of her heavy tail.
>
> (385)

As the story progresses, the manner of description becomes even less precise and much more poetic. When Mr Hancock wonders "how to keep his new found mermaid", he knows that "this phenomenon cannot be explained by science" and is overwhelmed by a feeling of melancholy he experienced looking into the vat: "as if a huge void were opening up where before all was solid and dull" (391). It is also Captain Jones who resorts to metaphors when he describes the eerie influence the mermaid has on the people around her: "[i]t was as if every soul on the ship knew that somewhere in the world there was a great love just for them. But that the world was so large that they would never find it" (385). The workers at the whaling dock think that the outbuildings where the vat with the mermaid is stored are haunted because they fall prey to the melancholy, too. They feel "ghastly sadness" that "comes off it, and can be felt within it" (396). Angelica also feels "some horrid miasma" when Mr Hancock moves the mermaid to a grotto near their new house: "[i]t taints her very lungs: some mornings it seems that all she breathes is grief" (408). The mermaid in captivity drains the life and joy of the people near her.

The more poetic description of the second mermaid might seem like a breach with empirically oriented realism, but in fact it evokes the early modern conviction that "imaginative fancy" capacitated "new forms of understanding" and figurative language helped to "define the [studied] phenomena".[43] The abandonment of the realist mode of writing enables a metaphorical description of the fate of women, which is signalled by the parallels that the author draws between mermaids and prostitutes. The first scene in which this is particularly evident is the scene of an orgy that Mrs Chappell prepares in her brothel as an event accompanying the exhibition of the carcass of the mermaid that she hired from Mr Hancock. Prostitutes disguised as sirens, with "skeins of chiffon hang[ing] from their wrists and float[ing] behind them" and "all the hair upon their mounds of pleasure" dyed as green as the moss that fringes a seaside rock-pool" (130), perform an erotic dance with men dressed up as sailors for the benefit of customers who pleasure themselves ogling the spectacle. The whole night has the qualities of phantasmagoria where the order of desire prevails over the order of reason. It is like a masquerade, which Terry Castle describes as a cultural phenomenon "imparting knowledge about the real world while giving access to a numinous realm of dream and taboo".[44]

Castle explains that modern bourgeois society is characterised by "rationalist taxonomies",[45] "a fear of ontological promiscuity and a desire for firm conceptual boundaries".[46] It scarcely tolerates "[a]mbiguous or hybrid form, forms that reach beyond themselves and are neither one thing nor another".[47] Masquerades, like carnivals, subvert the "fundamental logic of culture – the logic of categorical opposition".[48] It is not an accident then that a scene of masquerade, whose chief attraction is a creature transgressing the boundaries of species, appears early in the novel. It indicates the theme of the porousness of the conceptual distinctions used to describe the natural and social world in the eighteenth century. Angelica slips out of the role of a woman of ill repute into the role of an honest merchant's wife. Her friend is advanced from the position of a kept woman to that of a countess.

The mermaid symbolises then freedom from social constraints, which is nowhere more evident than in the life of prostitution. The comparison that Gowar draws between Angelica Neal and the marvellous creature entitles such an interpretation. "What she likes best [in whoredom] is to be desired. [...] She likes to be pursued, but she does not feel she is ever captured" (135). Angelica's subsequent wedding to Mr Hancock coincides with the moment her husband's acquisition of a living mermaid and her experience of married life is in a way a reflection of the state of the marvellous captive. Just like the mermaid can never be seen in her complete form while it is immersed in water, Angelica experiences her own identity as subject to fragmentation:

> More has slipped from her control than she had expected, and now she sees that as the months and years pass it will only slip further. She will never be simply her own self in the world again; the courtesan Angelica Neal, a personality all her own, is being parcelled up and claimed by connection upon connection. [...] These claims upon her will only multiply [...] and accordingly her own person will be divided and divided and divided until there is nothing left.
>
> (371)

The constraints of her new life correspond to the imprisonment of the mermaid in a vat in a grotto. Angelica feels as "hollow as a bleached shell" (405). The change in her appearance and behaviour is also noted by her husband who scarcely recognises her and experiences "the feeling of great loss, as if the soft and lavish wife he chose has already died and it is only her shell carrying on" (414).

It is only when Angelica decides to liberate the mermaid that she seems to regain control over her life and she becomes whole again. It is necessary to "give this beast its freedom" because as a "trapped creature" it cannot but "strike out" (477), she declares. With the help of her husband, she "take[s] her apart in buckets" and pour[s] it into a pool where "she swings in netty lengths, rediscovering her atomised self" (477). Similarly, Angelica reintegrates her identity, which will no longer be torn by the distinct social roles she has played in her life.

The party she organises to boast of her marvellous possession is the evidence of the sense of liberation she experiences. The list of guests reflects different stages of Angelica's career and different particles of her identity. "Mrs Hancock, lowborn, the plaything of aristocracy and wife of a gentleman merchant, has run wantonly riot with her own address book and drawn all to her in the name of Curiosity" (483). In an act of invalidation of social distinctions, she brings together people who, apart from very few occasions, move in very different circles, and creates an illusion of utopian reality:

> Even its members are surprised by one another, having been reasonably expected that a careful hostess takes pains to segregate her guests for the sake of delicacy, but they concede without a word spoken that this is really no different from any night at the pleasure

gardens, where those of all walks of life are thrown together and yet succeed in speaking to nobody outside their own sort.

(482)

The unexpected mingling of people from so distinct spheres at the mermaid party, which is "a most amphibious thing", sheds full light on the classification of Georgian world into discrete categories.

> In fact it might be observed the grotto becomes a very menagerie, a Wunderkammer of all the classifications human, who pace warily together, and watch with interest as each curiosity reveals its own habits as to feeding, and dancing, and drinking and conversation.

(482)

The hybrid creature, which attracted such diverse people, having been released by Mr and Mrs Hancock, is absent from the party. Angelica removes it then from the realm of empirical reality and sends it to the realm of dreams or fiction. Her guests may admire the mermaid's images in a beautifully decorated grotto but the marvel is an airy nothing without a local habitation. The very concept of the marvellous creature that contradicts the laws of nature, crossing the boundaries between species, evokes a utopian possibility of erasing social distinctions and releasing people from their assigned roles. "The vulgar quotidian is given no quarter here: all is beautiful and hazed as a dream" (484).

The conclusion of the novel may well be read as a metaphorical comment on the way the genre of the novel was refined of the conventions of writing that did not fit the epistemological or moral framework of the period. Angelica's conversion from a courtesan to a married woman is symbolic of the novel's shift to the description of domestic virtue. Mr and Mrs Hancock's liberation of the mermaid from their grotto and its return to the sea point to the realist turn of the novel and to the preservation of wonder only as a marvellous possibility and not a solid fact. The memory of Angelica's past and the illusion of the mermaid in her grotto, however, remain to remind the reader about the novelistic genre's miscegenated nature and its capacity to present reality in other ways than the literal.

By reviving the memory of diverse kinds of eighteenth-century fiction, *The Mermaid and Mrs. Hancock* offers a broad perspective on the familiar problems of the Georgian world and provides a critical commentary on the development of the novel. The use of noncanonical genres that exerted an influence on the formation of the novel exposes the heterogeneity of modes of living, thinking and writing in the eighteenth century and the artifice of the distinctions created in the culture of the period. The employment of motifs common in prostitute narratives brings to full light the life in the eighteenth-century underworld, of which the eighteenth-century canonical novelists could only offer occasional glimpses, and shows that in many respects it mirrored the principles of respectable social life. The use of the marvellous evokes the novel's affinity to Oriental fiction, in which fantasy and realism were regarded as equally legitimate means of the pursuit of truth about the world. Drawing on the fictional genres obliterated from the genealogy of the novel in order to recreate the Georgian world, Imogen Hermes Gowar restores the memory of the prehistory of the genre, uncovering the themes and conventions that have been removed from cultural memory in the process of its canonisation.

Notes

1 Linda Hutcheon, *A Poetics of Postmodernism: Theory, History and Fiction* (New York and London: Routledge,1988), x.
2 Roland Barthes, "The Reality Effect", in *The Rustle of Language*, ed. François Wahl, trans. Richard Howard (New York: Hill and Wang, 1986), 145.
3 Elodie Rousselot, "Introduction: Exoticising the Past in Contemporary Neo-Historical Fiction", in *Exoticizing the Past in Contemporary Neo-Historical Fiction*, ed. Elodie Rousselot (Houndmills: Palgrave Macmillan, 2014), 5.
4 "Authors at Foyles: Imogen Hermes Gowar", www.foyles.co.uk/author-imogen-hermes-gowar.
5 G.S. Rousseau and Roy Porter, "Preface", in *Exoticism in Enlightenment*, ed. G.S. Rousseau and Roy Porter (Manchester and New York: Manchester University Press, 1990), vi.
6 Srinivas Aravamudan, *Enlightenment Orientalism: Resisting the Rise of the Novel* (Chicago and London: The University of Chicago Press, 2012), 5.
7 Bradford K. Mudge, *The Whore's Story: Women, Pornography and the British Novel, 1684-1830* (Oxford: Oxford University Press, 2000), 23.
8 William Warner, *Licensing Entertainment: The Elevation of Novel Reading in Britain, 1684-1750* (Berkeley, Los Angeles and London: University of California Press, 1998), 43.
9 Warner, *Licensing Entertainment*, 40.
10 Leah Orr, *Novel Ventures. Fiction and Print Culture in England, 1690-1730* (Charlottesville and London: University of Virginia Press, 2017), 4.
11 Thomas Keymer, "Introduction", in *Prose Fiction in English From the Origins of Print to 1750*, ed. Thomas Keymer (Oxford: Oxford University Press, 2017), xxiii.
12 Srinivas Aravamudan, "Fiction/Translation/Transnation: The Secret History of the Eighteenth-Century Novel", in *A Companion to the*

Eighteenth-Century English Novel and Culture, ed. Paula R. Backscheider and Catherine Ingrassia (Malden: Blackwell Publishing, 2005), 49.

13 Mudge, *The Whore's Story*, 4.

14 Ian Watt, *The Rise of the Novel. Studies in Defoe, Richardson and Fielding* (1957; London: Penguin Books, 1972),14

15 Watt, *The Rise of the Novel*, 16

16 Watt, *The Rise of the Novel*, 11.

17 Sabor, "Introduction", in John Cleland, *Memoirs of a Woman of Pleasure*, ed. Peter Sabor (Oxford: Oxford University Press, 1985), vii.

18 Roy Porter, "Mixed Feelings: the Enlightenment and Sexuality in Eighteenth-Century Britain", in *Sexuality in Eighteenth-Century Britain*, ed. Paul-Gabriel Boycé (Manchester: Manchester University Press, 1982), 8.

19 Paul Baines, "Pornography and the Novel", in *The Oxford History of the Novel in English*. Volume 1. *Prose Fiction in English From the Origin of Print to 1750*, ed. Thomas Keymer (Oxford: Oxford University Press, 2017), 433.

20 Sabor, "Introduction", vii.

21 Sabor, "Introduction", xxii.

22 Daniel Defoe, *The Fortunes and Misfortunes of the Famous Moll Flanders* (1721), ed. Liz Bellamy, vol. 6 of *The Novels of Daniel Defoe*, ed. W. R. Owens and P.N. Furbank (London: Pickering and Chatto, 2009), 23.

23 Peter Stallybrass and Allan White, *The Politics and Poetics of Transgression* (Ithaca: Cornell University Press, 1986), 105.

24 Stallybrass and White, *The Politics and Poetics of Transgression*, 93.

25 Stallybrass and White, *The Politics and Poetics of Transgression*, 108.

26 Ann Lewis and Markman Ellis, "Introduction", in *Prostitution and Eighteenth-Century Culture: Sex, Commerce and Morality*, ed. Ann Lewis and Markman Ellis (2012; London and New York: Routledge, 2016), 1, 2.

27 Tony Henderson, *Disorderly Women in Eighteenth-Century London: Prostitution and Control in Metropolis 1730-1830* (London and New York: Longman, 1999), 194.

28 All the quotations from *The Mermaid and Mrs. Hancock* are from Imogen Hermes Gowar, *The Mermaid and Mrs. Hancock*. London: Vintage Books, 2018. Page numbers are included in parentheses.

29 Laura J. Rosenthal, *Infamous Commerce. Prostitution in Eighteenth-Century British Literature and Culture* (Ithaca and London: Cornell University Press, 2006), 2.

30 Laura J. Rosenthal, "Introduction", in *Nightwalkers: Prostitute Narratives from the Eighteenth Century*, ed. Laura J. Rosenthal (Peterborough: Broadview Press, 2000), xiii.

31 Rosenthal, *Infamous Commerce*, 3.

32 Rosenthal, "Introduction", xiv.

33 Rosenthal, "Introduction", xi.

34 Rosenthal, *Infamous Commerce*, 98.

35 Ros Ballaster, "Narrative Transmigrations: The Oriental Tale and the Novel in Eighteenth-Century Britain", in *A Companion to the Eighteenth-Century*

English Novel and Culture, ed. Paula R. Backscheider and Catherine Ingrassia (Malden: Blackwell Publishing, 2005), 75–76.

36 Jonathan Lamb, "Locke's Wild Fancies: Empiricism, Personhood, and Fictionality", *The Eighteenth Century* 48.3 (2007): 188.

37 Tita Chico, *The Experimental Imagination: Literary Knowledge and Science in the British Enlightenment* (Stanford: Stanford University Press, 2018), 1.

38 Sarah Tindal Kareem, *Eighteenth-Century Fiction and the Reinvention of Wonder* (New York: Oxford University Press, 2014), 2.

39 Katherine Binhammer, Eugenia Zuroski Jenkins, Daniel O'Quinn, Mary Helen McMurran and Srinivas Aravamudan, "Srinivas Aravamudan's *Enlightenment Orientalism: Resisting the Rise of the Novel*: A Roundtable Discussion", *Lumen* 33 (2014): 8.

40 Tzvetan Todorov, *A Structural Approach to a Literary Genre* (Ithaca: Cornell University Press, 1975), 55.

41 Robert Hooke, *Philosophical Experiment and Observations of the late Eminent Dr. Robert Hooke,* ed. William Derham (London, 1726), 21, quoted in Daniel Carey, "Inquiries, Heads and Directions: Orienting Early Modern Travel," in *Travel Narratives, the New Science, and Literary Discourse, 1569-1750*, ed. Judy A. Hayden (Farnham and Burlington: Ashgate, 2012), 46.

42 Jason H. Pearl, "Geography and Authority in the Royal Society's Instructions for Travelers", in *Travel Narratives, the New Science, and Literary Discourse, 1569-1750*, ed. Judy A Hayden (Farnham and Burlington: Ashgate, 2012), 71.

43 Chico, *The Experimental Imagination*, 1.

44 Terry Castle, *Masquerade and Civilization: The Carnivalesque in Eighteenth-Century English Culture and Fiction* (Stanford: Stanford University Press, 1986), 86.

45 Castle, *Masquerade and Civilization*, 107.

46 Castle, *Masquerade and Civilization*, 102.

47 Castle, *Masquerade and Civilization*, 103.

48 Castle, *Masquerade and Civilization*, 77.

Bibliography

Ackroyd, Peter. *Hawksmoor*. 1985. Harmondsworth: Penguin Books, 1993.

Ackroyd, Peter. *Chatterton*. 1987. Harmondsworth: Penguin Books, 1993.

Ackroyd, Peter. *Dan Leno and the Limehouse Golem*. London: Vintage, 1994.

Ackroyd, Peter. *London: The Biography*. 2000. London: Vintage, 2001.

Ackroyd, Peter. *The Lambs of London*. 2004. London: Vintage, 2005.

Ackroyd, Peter. *The History of England. Volume IV: Revolution*. 2016. London: Pan Books, 2017.

Addison, Joseph, *Critical Essays from the Spectator by Joseph Addison: with four Essays by Richard Steele*. Ed. D. F. Bond. Oxford: Oxford University Press, 1970.

Agamben, Giorgio. *Homo Sacer: Sovereign Power and Bare Life*. Trans. Daniel Heller-Roazen. Stanford: Stanford University Press, 1998.

Allan, David. *Commonplace Books and Reading in Georgian England*. Cambridge: Cambridge University Press, 2010.

Aravamudan, Srinivas. "Fiction/Translation/Transnation: The Secret History of the Eighteenth-Century Novel". In Paula R. Backscheider and Catherine Ingrassia (eds.), *A Companion to the Eighteenth-Century English Novel and Culture*. Malden: Blackwell Publishing, 2005. 48–74.

Aravamudan, Srinivas. *Enlightenment Orientalism: Resisting the Rise of the Novel*. Chicago and London: The University of Chicago Press, 2012.

Attridge, Derek. *J. M. Coetzee and the Ethics of Reading*. Chicago and London: University of Chicago Press, 2004.

Attridge, Derek. "Oppressive Silence: J. M. Coetzee's *Foe* and the Politics of Canonisation". In Graham Huggan and Stephen Watson (eds.), *Critical Perspectives on J. M. Coetzee*. Basingstoke and London: Macmillan, 1996. 168–190.

"Authors at Foyles: Imogen Hermes Gowar", www.foyles.co.uk/author-imogen-hermes-gowar.

Baines, Paul. "Pornography and the Novel". In Thomas Keymer (ed.), *Prose Fiction in English From the Origin of Print to 1750. The Oxford History of the Novel in English*. Volume 1. Oxford: Oxford University Press, 2017. 417–434.

Ballaster, Ros. "Narrative Transmigrations: The Oriental Tale and the Novel in Eighteenth- Century Britain". In Paula R. Backscheider and Catherine

Ingrassia (eds.), *A Companion to the Eighteenth-Century English Novel and Culture*. Malden: Blackwell Publishing, 2005. 75–96.

Ballaster, Ros. *Seductive Forms. Women's Amatory Fiction from 1684 to 1740*. Oxford: Oxford University Press, 2007.

Ballaster, Ros. "The Rise and Decline of the Epistolary Novel, 1770-1832". In J. A. Downie (ed.), *The Oxford Handbook of The Eighteenth-Century Novel*. Oxford: Oxford University Press, 2016. 409–425.

Barker, Francis and Peter Hulme. "Nymphs and Reapers Heavily Vanish: The Discursive Con-texts of *The Tempest*". In John Drakakis (ed.), *Alternative Shakespeares*. London and New York: Routledge, 2005.

Barthes, Roland. "The Reality Effect". In *The Rustle of Language*. Ed. François Wahl. Trans. Richard Howard. New York: Hill and Wang, 1986. 141–148.

Bataille, Georges. *Death and Sensuality: Eroticism and Taboo*. Trans. Mary Dalwood. New York: Walker and Company, 1962.

Bataille, Georges. *Inner Experience*. Trans. Leslie Anne Boldt. Albany: State University of New York Press, 1988.

Baudrillard, Jean. *Simulacra and Simulation*. 1981. Trans. Sheila Faria Glaser. Ann Arbor: University of Michigan Press, 2008.

Begam, Richard. "Silence and Mut(e)ilation: White Writing in J. M. Coetzee's *Foe*". *The South Atlantic Quarterly* 93.1 (1994): 111–129.

Berhoz, Alain. *The Vicarious Brain, Creator of Worlds*. Trans. Giselle Weiss. Cambridge, MA and London: Harvard University Press, 2017.

Bhabha, Homi K. *The Location of Culture*. London and New York: Routledge, 2004.

Bindman, David. *Hogarth*. London: Thames and Hudson, 1981.

Binhammer, Katherine, Eugenia Zuroski Jenkins, Daniel O'Quinn, Mary Helen McMurran and Srinivas Aravamudan. "Srinivas Aravamudan's *Enlightenment Orientalism: Resisting the Rise of the Novel*: A Roundtable Discussion". *Lumen* 33 (2014): 1–26.

Biography of Chatterton. 2014. The Thomas Chatterton Society. <www. thomaschattertonsociety.com/#!biography/cee5>

Bolla, Peter, de. *The Education of the Eye: Painting, Landscape, and Architecture in Eighteenth-Century Britain*. Stanford: Stanford University Press, 2003.

Bongie, Chris. "'Lost in the Maze of Doubting': J. M. Coetzee's *Foe* and the Politics of (Un)likeness". *Modern Fiction Studies* 39.2 (1993): 261–281.

Boulukos, George. *The Grateful Slave: The Emergence of Race in Eighteenth-Century British and American Culture*. Cambridge: Cambridge University Press, 2008.

Brantly, Susan C. "Engaging the Enlightenment. Tournier's *Friday*, Delblanc's *Speranza*, and Unsworth's *Sacred Hunger*". *Comparative Literature* 61.2 (2009): 128–141.

Brindle, Kym. *Epistolary Encounters in Neo-Victorian Fiction: Diaries and Letters*. Houndmills: Palgrave Macmillan, 2013.

Brown, Laura. "Pope and the Other". In Pat Rogers (ed.), *The Cambridge Companion to Alexander Pope*. Cambridge: Cambridge University Press, 2007. 222–236.

Budakov, Vesselin M., Jonathan McCreedy and Alexandra K. Glavanakova. "Introduction". In Jonathan McCreedy, Vesselin M. Budakov and Alexandra K. Glavanakova (eds.), *The Legacy of Jonathan Swift from the Enlightenment to the Age of Post-Truth*. Newcastle: Cambridge Scholars Publishing, 2020. ix–xx.

Campbell, Stuart. *Daniel Defoe's Railway Journey: A Surreal Odyssey through Modern Britain*. Dingwall: Sandstone Press, 2017.

Carey, Brycchan and Sarah Salih. "Introduction". In Brycchan Carey, Markman Ellis and Sarah Salih (eds.), *Discourses of Slavery and Abolition. Britain and Its Colonies, 1760-1838*. Houndmills: Palgrave Macmillan, 2004. 1–8.

Carey, Daniel. "Inquiries, Heads and Directions: Orienting Early Modern Travel". In Judy A. Hayden (ed.), *Travel Narratives, the New Science, and Literary Discourse, 1569-1750*. Farnham and Burlington: Ashgate, 2012. 25–51.

Carter, Linda. "Contaminated Copies: J. M. Coetzee's *Foe*". In Madelena Gonzalez and Marie-Odile Pittin-Hédon (eds.), *Generic Instability and Identity in the Contemporary Novel*. Newcastle: Cambridge Scholars Publishing, 2010. 26–33.

Carusi, Annamaria. "*Foe*: The Narrative and Power", *Journal of Literary Studies* 5.2 (1989): 134–144.

Castle, Terry. *Masquerade and Civilization: The Carnivalesque in Eighteenth-Century English Culture and Fiction*. Stanford: Stanford University Press, 1986.

Castle, Terry. *The Female Thermometer: Eighteenth-Century Culture and the Invention of the Uncanny*. Oxford: Oxford University Press, 1995.

Charles, Marilyn. *The Stories We Live: Psychoanalysis and Literature*. Lanham: Rowman & Littlefield, 2015.

Chico, Tita. *The Experimental Imagination: Literary Knowledge and Science in the British Enlightenment*. Stanford: Stanford University Press, 2018.

Clark, Robert. "Robinsonade and Brexit: Free Trade, Empire and the Whole World". In Emanuelle Peraldo (ed.), *300 Years of Robinsonades*. Newcastle: Cambridge Scholars Publishing, 2020. 165–189.

Coetzee, J. M. *Foe*. 1986. London: Penguin Books, 2010.

Coetzee, J. M. "Roads to Translation". *Tongues: Translation: Only Connect* 64.4 (2005): 141–151.

Coetzee, J. M. *Stranger Shores: Essays 1986-1999*. London: Vintage, 2002.

Cook, Daniel. *Thomas Chatterton and Neglected Genius, 1760-1830*. Houndmills: Palgrave Macmillan, 2013.

Corcoran, Patrick. "*Foe*: Metafiction and the Discourse of Power". In Lieve Spaas and Brian Stimpson (eds.), *Robinson Crusoe: Myths and Metamorphoses*. London: Macmillan; New York: St Martin's, 1996. 256–266.

Cowart, David. *Literary Symbiosis: The Reconfigured Text in Twentieth-Century Writing*. Athens, GA and London: University of Georgia Press, 1993.

Cryle, Peter and Lisa O'Connel (eds.). *Libertine Enlightenment: Sex, Liberty and License in the Eighteenth Century*. Houndmills: Palgrave Macmillan, 2003.

Dabydeen, David. *Hogarth, Walpole and Commercial Britain*. London: Hansib, 1987.

Dabydeen, David. *Hogarth's Blacks: Images of Blacks in Eighteenth-Century English Art*. Manchester: Manchester University Press, 1987.

Dabydeen, David. *A Harlot's Progress*. 1999. London: Vintage, 2000.

Davenant, William and John Dryden. *The Tempest, Or the Enchanted Island. A Comedy*. London: Company, 1720.

Dean, Michael. *I, Hogarth*. New York and London: Overlook Duckworth, 2012.

Dean, Michael, "William Hogarth and Georgian Life". *History Today* 62.10 (October 2012). www.historytoday.com/william-hogarth-and-georgian-life.

Defoe, Daniel. *Serious Reflections During the Life and Surprising Adventures of Robinson Crusoe*. London: W. Taylor, 1720.

Defoe, Daniel. *A Tour through the Whole Island of Great Britain*. 1724-1726. Ed. Pat Rogers. Harmondsworth: Penguin Books, 1971.

Defoe, Daniel. *Robinson Crusoe*. 1719. Ed. Michael Shinagel. 2nd edition. New York and London: W. W. Norton, 1994.

Defoe, Daniel. *Roxana, The Fortunate Mistress*. 1724. Ed. John Mullan. Oxford: Oxford University Press, 2008.

Defoe, Daniel. *The Fortunes and Misfortunes of the Famous Moll Flanders* (1721). Ed. Liz Bellamy. *The Novels of Daniel Defoe*. Ed. W. R. Owens and P.N. Furbank. Vol. 6. London: Pickering and Chatto, 2009.

Effe, Alexandra. *J. M. Coetzee and the Ethics of Narrative Transgression*. Cham: Palgrave Macmillan, 2017.

Ellis, Markman. *The Politics of Slavery: Race, Gender and Commerce in the Sentimental Novel*. Cambridge: Cambridge University Press, 1996.

Engélibert, Jean-Paul. "Daniel Defoe as Character: Subversion of the Myths of Robinson Crusoe and of the Author". In Lieve Spaas and Brian Stimpson (eds.), *Robinson Crusoe: Myths and Metamorphoses*. London: Macmillan; New York: St Martin's, 1996. 267–281.

Faurholt, Gry. "Self as Other: The Doppelgänger". *Double Dialogues* 10 (2009). <www.doubledialogues.com/article/self-as-other-the-doppelganger/>

Fielding, Henry. *The Masquerade, A Poem Inscribed to C---T H--D--G--R*. London: J. Roberts, A. Dodd, 1728.

Fisher, Mark. *Ghosts of My Life: Writings on Depression, Hauntology and Lost Futures*. Winchester and Washington: Zero Books, 2014.

Fokkema, Aleid. "The Author: Postmodernism's Stock Character". In Paul Franssen and Ton Hoenselaars (eds.), *The Author as Character: Representing Historical Writers in Western Literature*. London: Associated University Presses, 1999. 39–51.

Forter, Greg. "Barry Unsworth and the Arts of Power: Historical Memory, Utopian Fictions". *Contemporary Literature* 51.4 (2011): 777–809.

Forter, Greg. *Critique and Utopia in Postcolonial Historical Fiction: Atlantic and Other Worlds*. Oxford and New York: Oxford University Press, 2019.

Foucault, Michel. *Discipline and Punish: The Birth of the Prison*. New York: Vintage Books, 1995.

Fowler, Elizabeth. "The Ship Adrift". In Peter Hulme and William H. Sherman (eds.), *The Tempest and Its Travels*. London: Reaktion Books, 2000. 37–40.

Franssen, Paul and Ton Hoenselaars (eds.). *The Author as Character: Representing Historical Writers in Western Literature*. London: Associated University Presses, 1999.

Gandelman, Claude. *Reading Pictures, Viewing Texts*. Bloomington and Indiana: Indiana University Press, 1991.

Ganofsky, Marine. *Night in French Libertine Fiction*. Oxford: Voltaire Foundation, 2018.

Gardam, Jane. *Crusoe's Daughter*. London: Abacus, 1985.

Gibson, Jeremy and Julian Wolfreys. *Peter Ackroyd: The Ludic and Labyrinthine Text*. Houndmills: Palgrave Macmillan, 2000.

Gildon, Charles. *The Life and Strange Surprizing Adventures of Mr. D— De F—, of London, Hosier*. London: J. Roberts, 1719.

Gilmour, Robin. "Using the Victorians: the Victorian Age in Contemporary Fiction". In Alice Jenkins and Juliet John (eds.), *Rereading Victorian Fiction*. Houndmills: Palgrave Macmillan, 2002. 189–200.

Gowar, Imogenes Hermes. *The Mermaid and Mrs. Hancock*. London: Vintage Books, 2018.

Griffin, Nicholas. *The House of Sight and Shadow*. London: Abacus, 2000.

Grimes, Ronald L. "Masking: Toward a Phenomenology of Exteriorization". *Journal of the American Academy of Religion* 43 (1975): 508–516.

Groot, Jerome, de. "Transgression and Experimentation: The Historical Novel". In Peter Boxall (ed.), *The Cambridge Companion to British Fiction: 1980-2018*. Cambridge: Cambridge University Press, 2018. 169–184.

Hadley, Louisa. *Neo-Victorian Fiction and Historical Narrative: The Victorians and Us*. Houndmills: Palgrave Macmillan, 2010.

Hagstrum, Jean H. *The Sister Arts: The Tradition of Literary Pictorialism and English Poetry from Dryden to Gray*. Chicago: University of Chicago Press, 1958.

Hallett, Mark. *The Spectacle of Difference: Graphic Satire in the Age of Hogarth*. New Haven: Yale University Press, 1999.

Harvey, A. D. *Sex in Georgian England*. London: Phoenix, 2001.

Head, Dominic. *J. M. Coetzee. 1997*. Cambridge: Cambridge University Press, 2010.

Heiland, Donna. "Historical Subjects: Recent Fiction about the Eighteenth Century". *Eighteenth-Century Life* 21 (1997): 108–122.

Heilmann, Ann and Mark Llewellyn. *Neo-Victorianism: The Victorians in the Twenty-First Century*. Houndmills: Palgrave Macmillan, 2010.

Henderson, Tony. *Disorderly Women in Eighteenth-Century London: Prostitution and Control in Metropolis, 1730-1830*. London and New York: Longman, 1999.

Hogarth, William. *The Analysis of Beauty*. Ed. Ronald Paulson. New Haven and London: Yale University Press, 1997.

Horkheimer, Max and Theodor W. Adorno. *Dialectic of Enlightenment:*
Philosophical Fragments. 1944. Ed. Gunzelin Schmid Noer. Trans. Edmund
Jephcott. Stanford: Stanford University Press, 2002.

Hudson, Nicholas. *"Tom Jones".* In Claude Rawson (ed.), *The Cambridge*
Companion to Henry Fielding. Cambridge: Cambridge University Press,
2007. 80–93.

Hutcheon, Linda. *The Poetics of Postmodernism: History, Theory, Fiction.* 1988.
New York and London: Routledge, 2004.

Hutcheon, Linda. *A Theory of Adaptation.* London: Routledge, 2006.

Irwin, Michael. *The Skull and the Nightingale.* London: Blue Door, 2013.

Jameson, Fredric. *Postmodernism, or, the Cultural Logic of Late Capitalism.*
London and New York: Verso, 2008.

Janssens-Knorsch, Uta and Hans-Christof Graf von Nayhauss. "Panorama
Europy (Druga połowa XVIII wieku)". In Annick Benoit-Dusausoy and
Guy Fontaine (eds.), *Literatura Europy: Historia Literatury Europejskiej.*
Trans. Elżbieta Skibińska et al. Gdańsk: słowo/obraz terytoria, 2009.
472–502.

Jay, Martin. *Songs of Experience. Modern American and European Variations on*
a Universal Theme. Berkeley: University of California Press, 2005.

Jones, Radhika. "Father-Born: Mediating the Classics in J. M. Coetzee's *Foe".*
Digital Defoe 1.1 (2009): 45–69.

Kaplan, Cora. *Victoriana: Histories, Fiction, Criticism.* Edinburgh: Edinburgh
University Press, 2007.

Kareem, Sarah Tindal. *Eighteenth-Century Fiction and the Reinvention of*
Wonder. New York: Oxford University Press, 2014.

Keymer, Thomas. "Introduction". In Thomas Keymer (ed.), *Prose Fiction in*
English From the Origins of Print to 1750. The Oxford History of the Novel in
English. Volume 1. Oxford: Oxford University Press, 2017. xvii–xxxi.

Keymer, Tom. "Slave and whore". *The Times Literary Supplement* (7 May
1999). 22.

Kohlke, Marie-Luise. "Introduction: Speculations in and on the Neo-Victorian
Encounter". *Neo-Victorian Studies* 1.1 (2008): 1–18.

Kotte, Christina. *Ethical Dimensions in British Historiographic Metafiction:*
Julian Barnes, Graham Swift, Penelope Lively. Trier: WVT, 2001.

Lackey, Michael (ed.). *Biographical Fiction: A Reader.* London and New York:
Bloomsbury, 2017.

Lamb, Jonathan. "Locke's Wild Fancies: Empiricism, Personhood, and
Fictionality". *The Eighteenth Century* 48.3 (2007): 187–204.

Lewis, Ann and Markman Ellis. "Introduction". In Ann Lewis and Markman
Ellis (eds.), *Prostitution and Eighteenth-Century Culture: Sex, Commerce and*
Morality. 2012. London and New York: Routledge, 2016. 1–16.

Lipski, Jakub. *In Quest of the Self: Masquerade and Travel in the Eighteenth-*
Century Novel. Fielding, Smollett, Sterne. Amsterdam and New York:
Rodopi, 2014.

Lipski, Jakub. *Painting the Novel: Pictorial Discourse in Eighteenth-Century*
English Fiction. London and New York: Routledge, 2018.

Locke, John. *An Essay concerning Human Understanding*. Ed. Peter H. Nidditch. Oxford: Oxford University Press, 1975.

Lodge, David. *Small World: An Academic Romance*. London: Penguin Books, 1985.

Loomba, Ania. *Colonialism/Postcolonialism*. London and New York: Routledge, 2015.

Lopez, Maria. *"Foe*: A Ghost Story". *Journal of Commonwealth Literature* 45.2 (2010): 295–310.

Lubey, Kathleen. *Excitable Imaginations: Eroticism and Reading in Britain, 1660-1760*. Lewisburg: Bucknell University Press, 2012.

Macaskill, Brian and Jeanne Colleran. "Reading History, Writing Heresy: The Resistance of Representation and the Representation of Resistance in J. M. Coetzee's *Foe*". *Contemporary Literature* 33.3 (1992): 432–457.

MacLeod, Lewis. "'Do We of Necessity Become Puppets in a Story?' or Narrating the World: On Speech, Silence, and Discourse in J. M. Coetzee's *Foe*". *Modern Fiction Studies* 52.1 (2006): 1–18.

Maher, Susan Naramore. "Confronting Authority: J. M. Coetzee's *Foe* and the Remaking of *Robinson Crusoe*". *The International Fiction Review* 18.1 (1991): 34–40.

Malandain, Pierre. "Panorama Europy (Pierwsza połowa XVIII wieku. Oświecenie)". In Annick Benoit-Dusausoy and Guy Fontaine (eds.), *Literatura Europy: Historia Literatury Europejskiej*. Trans. Elżbieta Skibińska et al. Gdańsk: słowo/obraz terytoria, 2009. 410–452.

Malone, Edmund. *An Inquiry into the Authenticity of Certain Miscellaneous Papers and Legal Instruments Attributed to Shakspeare*. 1769. London: T. Cadell, Jun. and W. Davies, 1796.

Mantel, Hilary. "Guilt around the Pictureframe". *The Independent* (22 May 1999). www.independent.co.uk/arts-entertainment/books-guilt-around-the-picture-frame-a-harlots-progress-by-david-dabydeen-jonathan-cape-pounds-10-1095106.html.

Marais, M. J. "The Deployment of Metafiction in an Aesthetics of Engagement in J. M. Coetzee's *Foe*". *Journal of Literary Studies* 5.2 (1989): 183–193.

Marshall, David. "Autobiographical Acts in *Robinson Crusoe*". *ELH* 71.3 (2004): 899–920.

Marshall, David. *The Frame of Art: Fictions of Aesthetic Experience, 1750–1815*. Baltimore: Johns Hopkins University Press, 2005.

Marshall, David and Dean Mace. "Literature and the Other Arts". In H. B. Nisbet and Claude Rawson (eds.), *The Cambridge History of Literary Criticism: The Eighteenth Century*, vol. 4. Cambridge: Cambridge University Press, 1997; online, 2008), 681–674.

Marx, Karl. *Capital: A Critique of Political Economy. Volume One*. Trans. Ben Fowkes. London and New York: Penguin Books, 1990.

Mayer, Robert. *History and the Early English Novel: Matters of Fact from Bacon to Defoe*. 1997. Cambridge: Cambridge University Press, 2004.

McHale, Brian. *Postmodernist Fiction*. 1987. London and New York: Routledge, 1991.

Mee, Jonathan. "Libertines and Radicals in the 1790s: The Strange Case of Charles Pigott I". In Peter Cryle and Lisa O'Connel (eds.), *Libertine Enlightenment: Sex, Liberty and License in the Eighteenth Century.* Houndmills: Palgrave Macmillan, 2003. 185–203.

Mitchell, Kate. *History and Cultural Memory in Neo-Victorian Fiction: Victorian Afterimages.* Houndmills: Palgrave Macmillan, 2010.

Mitchell, Kate and Nicola Parson. "Reading the Represented Past: History and Fiction from 1700 to the Present". In Kate Mitchell and Nicola Parson (eds.), *Reading Historical Fiction: The Revenant and Remembered Past.* Houndmills: Palgrave Macmillan, 2013. 1–18.

Moore, John Robert. *Daniel Defoe: Citizen of the Modern World.* Chicago: University of Chicago Press, 1958.

Moore, Stephen. *The Novel: An Alternative History, 1600-1800.* New York: Continuum, 2010.

More, Hannah. *Slavery: A Poem.* London: Printed for T. Cadell, 1788.

Morgan, Kenneth. *Slavery and the British Empire: From Africa to America.* Oxford and New York: Oxford University Press, 2007.

Mudge, Bradford K. *The Whore's Story: Women, Pornography and the British Novel, 1684-1830.* Oxford: Oxford University Press, 2000.

Mudge, Bradford K. (ed.). *When Flesh Becomes Word: An Anthology of Early Eighteenth-Century Libertine Literature.* Oxford: Oxford University Press, 2004.

Newman, Judie. "Desperately Seeking Susan: J. M. Coetzee, *Robinson Crusoe* and *Roxana*". *Current Writing* 6.1 (1994): 1–12.

Norman, Diana. *Shores of Darkness.* 1996. London: Penguin Books, 1997.

Novak, Maximillian E. (ed.). *English Literature in the Age of Disguise.* Berkeley: University of California Press, 1977.

Onega, Susana. *Metafiction and Myth in the Novels of Peter Ackroyd.* Columbia: Camden House, 1999.

Orr, Leah. *Novel Ventures: Fiction and Print Culture in England, 1690-1730.* Charlottesville and London: University of Virginia Press, 2017.

Parker, Jo Alyson. "Crusoe's *Foe*, Foe's *Cruso*, and the Origins and Future of the Novel". *KronoScope* 11.1–2 (2011): 17–40.

Paulson, Ronald, *Hogarth: His Life, Art, and Times.* Abr. Anne Wilde. New Haven and London: Yale University Press, 1974.

Paulson, Ronald. *Hogarth: The "Modern Moral Subject" 1607-1732.* New Brunswick and London: Rutgers University Press, 1991.

Pearl, Jason H. "Geography and Authority in the Royal Society's Instructions for Travelers". In Judy A Hayden (ed.), *Travel Narratives, the New Science, and Literary Discourse, 1569-1750.* Farnham and Burlington: Ashgate, 2012. 71–83.

Peterson, Christopher. "The Home of Friday: Coetzee's *Foe*". *Textual Practice* 30.5 (2016): 857–877.

Porter, Roy. "Mixed Feelings: the Enlightenment and Sexuality in Eighteenth-Century Britain". In Paul-Gabriel Boycé (ed.), *Sexuality in Eighteenth-Century Britain.* Manchester: Manchester University Press, 1982. 1–27.

Porter, Roy. *Enlightenment: Britain and the Creation of the Modern World*. London: Penguin Books, 2001, Apple books edition.

Rediker, Marcus. *The Slave Ship: A Human History*. London: Viking Penguin, 2007.

Rediker, Marcus. *Outlaws of the Atlantic: Sailors, Pirates, and Motley Crews in the Age of Sail*. Boston: Beacon Press, 2014.

Richardson, Samuel. *Pamela, or, Virtue Rewarded*. 1740. London: Cock and McGowan, 1816.

Robinson, Alan. *Narrating the Past. Historiography, Memory and the Contemporary Novel*. Houndmills: Palgrave Macmillan, 2011.

Rosenberger, Diana. "Virtual Rewarded: What #MeToo Can Learn from Samuel Richardson's *Pamela*". *South Central Review* 36.2 (2019): 17-32.

Rosenthal, Laura J. "Introduction". In *Nightwalkers: Prostitute Narratives from the Eighteenth Century*. Ed. Laura J. Rosenthal. Peterborough: Broadview Press, 2000. ix–xx.

Rosenthal, Laura. *Infamous Commerce. Prostitution in Eighteenth-Century British Literature and Culture*. Ithaca and London: Cornell University Press, 2006.

Rousseau, G. S. "Ingenious Pain: Fiction, History, Biography, and the Miraculous Eighteenth Century". *Eighteenth Century Life* 25 (2001): 47–62.

Rousseau, G.S. and Roy Porter. "Preface". In G. S. Rousseau and Roy Porter (eds.), *Exoticism in Enlightenment*. Manchester and New York: Manchester University Press, 1990. vi–x.

Rousselot, Elodie. *Exoticising the Past in Contemporary Neo-Historical Fiction*. Houndmills: Palgrave Macmillan, 2014.

Rousselot, Elodie. "Introduction: Exoticising the Past in Contemporary Neo-Historical Fiction". In Elodie Rousselot (ed.), *Exoticizing the Past in Contemporary Neo-Historical Fiction*. Houndmills: Palgrave Macmillan, 2014. 1–16.

Ryba, Janusz. *Maskarady oświeconych: Próba opisu zjawiska*. Katowice: Wydawnictwo Uniwersytetu Śląskiego, 1998.

Ryba, Janusz. *Oświeceniowe tutti frutti: Maskarady – konwersacja – literatura*. Katowice: Wydawnictwo Uniwersytetu Śląskiego, 2009.

Sabor, Peter. "Introduction". In John Cleland, *Memoirs of a Woman of Pleasure*. Ed. Peter Sabor. Oxford: Oxford University Press, 1985. vii–xxv.

Sachs, Jonathan. "The Future of the Eighteenth Century". *The Rambling* 9 (2020). https://the-rambling.com/2020/08/07/issue9-sachs/.

Savu, Laura E. *Postmortem Postmodernists: The Afterlife of the Author in Recent Narrative*. Madison: Fairleigh Dickinson Press, 2009.

Sexton, David. "Thereby Hangs a Tale: *Dan Leno and the Limehouse Golem* by Peter Ackroyd". *The Spectator* 8670 (1994).

Shakespeare, William. *The Tempest*. 1611. Ed. Burton Raffel. New Haven and London: Yale University Press, 2006.

Shields, M. Kathryn. "The Drama of Identity: Masking and Evolving Notions of Self in Contemporary Photography". In Deborah Bell (ed.), *Masquerade:*

Essays on Tradition and Innovation Worldwide. Jefferson: McFarland, 2015. 196–214.

Shiller, Dana. "The Redemptive Past in the Neo-Victorian Novel". *Studies in the Novel* 29.4 (1997): 538–560.

Shuttleworth, Sally. "Natural History: The Retro-Victorian Novel". In Elinor S. Shaffer (ed.), *The Third Culture: Literature and Science.* Berlin and New York: Walter de Gruyter, 1998. 253–267.

Shuttleworth, Sally. "From Retro- to Neo-Victorian Fiction and Beyond: Fearful Symmetries". In Nadine Boehm-Schnitker and Susanne Gruss (eds.), *Neo-Victorian Literature and Culture: Immersions and Revisitations.* London and New York: Routledge, 2014. 179–192.

Smith, Chloe Wigston. "How harassed women had their #MeToo moments in the 18th century". *The Conversation* (26 February 2018). https://theconversation.com/how-harassed-women-had-their-metoo-moments-in-the-18th-century-91761.

Smolderen, Thierry. *The Origins of Comics: From William Hogarth to Winsor McCay.* Jackson: University Press of Mississippi, 2014.

Smollett, Tobias. *The Adventures of Roderick Random.* London, New York and Toronto: Oxford University Press, 1952.

Spivak, Gayatri Chakravorty. "Theory in the Margin: Coetzee's *Foe* Reading Defoe's *Crusoe/Roxana*". *English in Africa* 17.2 (1990): 1–23.

Stallybrass, Peter and Allan White. *The Politics and Poetics of Transgression.* Ithaca: Cornell University Press, 1986.

Stevens, Anne H. *British Historical Fiction before Scott.* Houndmills: Palgrave Macmillan, 2010.

Strehle, Susan. "Rewriting Darkness: Imperial Knowledge in Barry Unsworth's *Sacred Hunger*". *Studies in the Novel* 43.1 (2011): 75–93.

Thomson, James. *The Seasons*, ed. James Sambrook. Oxford: Clarendon, 1981.

Todorov, Tzvetan. *A Structural Approach to a Literary Genre.* Ithaca: Cornell University Press, 1975.

Turk, Tisha. "Intertextuality and the Collaborative Construction of Narrative: J. M. Coetzee's *Foe*". *Narrative* 19.3 (2013): 295–310.

Uglow, Jenny. *Hogarth: A Life and a World.* London: Faber, 1997.

Unsworth, Barry. *Sacred Hunger.* London: Penguin Books, 1992.

Voogd, Peter Jan, de. *Henry Fielding and William Hogarth: The Correspondences of the Arts.* Amsterdam: Rodopi, 1981.

Wahrman, Dror. *The Making of the Modern Self: Identity and Culture in Eighteenth-Century England.* Yale: Yale University Press, 2004.

Ward, Abigail, "David Dabydeen's *A Harlot's Progress*". *Journal of Postcolonial Writing* 43.1 (2007): 32–44.

Warner, William. *Licensing Entertainment: The Elevation of Novel Reading in Britain, 1684–1750.* Berkeley, Los Angeles and London: University of California Press, 1998.

Watt, Ian. *The Rise of the Novel. Studies in Defoe, Richardson and Fielding.* 1957. Harmondsworth: Penguin Books, 1972.

Webster, Jeremy W. *Performing Libertinism in Charles II's Court: Politics, Drama, Sexuality.* Houndmills: Palgrave Macmillan, 2005.

Wendorf, Richard (ed.). *Articulate Images: The Sister Arts from Hogarth to Tennyson.* Minneapolis: University of Minnesota Press, 1983.

Williams, Abigail. *The Social Life of Books: Reading Together in the Eighteenth-Century Home.* New Haven and London: Yale University Press, 2017.

Wu, Kai-su. "Decomposing the Authoritative Author: Truth and Confession in J. M. Coetzee's *Foe* and *Summertime*". *Tamkang Review* 43.2 (2013): 107–129.

Wulf, Andrea. "A Rake's Progress". *New York Times* (1 February 2013). www.nytimes.com/2013/02/03/books/review/i-hogarth-by-michael-dean.html.

Index